A GIFT FOR:

. . . .

FROM:

. . . .

DATE:

. . . .

THE FORGIVENESS JOURNAL

A Guided Journey to Forgiving What You Can't Forget

[handwritten notes: 3159614 / Comaka@123 / Lunarleo]

LYSA TERKEURST

THOMAS NELSON®
Since 1798

The Forgiveness Journal

© 2020 Haven Place Ministries

A portion of the text in this book was taken from Forgiving What You Can't Forget © 2020 Lysa TerKeurst.

Published in Nashville, Tennessee, by Thomas Nelson. Thomas Nelson is a registered trademark of HarperCollins Christian Publishing, Inc.

Photos by Kelsie Gorham

Supplemental text written by Carrie Marrs

Special thanks to the following for their contributions to this journal:

Amanda Bacon	Joel Muddamalle	Kimberly Henderson
Leah Chabai	Shae Tate	Meredith Brock

Thomas Nelson titles may be purchased in bulk for educational, business, fund-raising, or sales promotional use. For information, please email SpecialMarkets@ThomasNelson.com.

ISBN: 978-1-4002-2438-8

Printed in China

22 23 24 25 26 GRI 11 10 9 8 7 6

CONTENTS

WORKING THROUGH FORGIVENESS TOGETHER

DEAR FRIEND, WELCOME to a safe space. I'm so glad you're meeting with me here.

Maybe you picked up this journal because you're going through one of the most difficult seasons you've ever walked through. Your life seems to be defined by a series of events that has changed everything for you. Or maybe you're addressing a traumatic part of your past you can't avoid anymore. Or perhaps you've just been living with a general unsettledness and heaviness related to unresolved hurts.

I know you may be having some incredibly raw emotions. You might feel angry, unfairly treated, or paralyzed by pain. Or maybe a lot of those feelings are buried. You seem to be doing all right for the most part. Yes, every now and then strong feelings rise to the surface. But honestly, you don't really want those feelings to reveal something else that needs to be tended to, talked about, dealt with, or forgiven.

Whatever the details of your situation, if you feel stuck with circumstances and feelings you can't control, I understand. If you're at an utter loss at how to take even a tiny step forward from where you are today. If you feel scared that you're hurting too much to ever be healed enough to see beautiful again.

I get all of that. I really do. I have felt a combination of all those things.

And for me, working through those thoughts and feelings, and processing the pain tangled with them, took time. So much time.

Journaling became critical for me as I was writing *Forgiving What You Can't Forget.* In the beginning, I was just working on

a book. Then it became very apparent that I needed a place to write and process all I was learning and feeling. So that's where the idea for this journal was born. I wanted you to have a place to work through everything just like I did.

But I also wanted to have a personal connection with you—a meeting place where we could come together in our journeys of forgiveness. All the pictures throughout this journal are of places that are special to me. You'll see where I've spent time while writing this message and doing the work of forgiveness in my personal life. I want to invite you into my home and to these other significant spots where I have hurt and been honest, wrestled and prayed, cried and wondered if I'd ever get through this, and then over time, found healing. I want you to come sit with me in these tender places. I want you to remember you are not alone.

If you were at my house, we'd be seated at my gray kitchen table breaking bread and sharing the stories that broke our hearts. And in the reality of shed tears and shared stories, we'd find that although our circumstances may be different, we are so very much alike. I'd hand you tissues and say, "I believe you" and "I'm so sorry." We'd keep opening our hearts and sharing and connecting as we took steps toward healing.

I want to do that with you as much as we can here in this journal.

Though we aren't actually seated at the gray table together today, I left a seat open for you. I knew that one day we'd process this message of forgiveness together—not only through reading the book but also through journaling our experiences.

I want you to have room to be yourself here. Processing can be messy, but when it gets us to healthier places, it's so worth it. Together we can move toward trusting God with our hearts and discovering the beauty He has for us.

We'll begin by just naming where we are. Any answer is okay. We're all bringing feelings to the gray table. We all come with issues to work through and feelings to sort out.

Describe some of the feelings of resistance, confusion, or fear you have about forgiving someone who has hurt you.

....

....

....

....

....

....

I want to assure you of something vitally important: You won't be judged as you wrestle through this message. I will not shame you for your struggle or blame you for your skepticism.

But, at the same time, I care about you too much and have tasted too much freedom and healing in my own life not to encourage you to do the hard work of forgiveness.

That's why I want to share what I've learned forgiveness *is* and *is not* right here at the beginning. We'll be talking about these throughout the book, but I pray that hearing these things early on will help you press past some of the doubts and questions that may be making you feel resistant to the idea of forgiveness.

1. *Forgiveness doesn't always fix relationships, but it does help mend the hurting heart.* Forgiveness is making the decision that the ones who hurt you no longer get to limit you, label you, or project the lies they believe about themselves onto you. It is the decision that their offense will not define you or confine you by the smallness of bitterness.

2. *Forgiveness is both a decision and a process, and healing is a long journey.* When you get triggered, it does not mean your decision to forgive was fake. It just means there's more to be done. Your decision to forgive the facts of what happened is done in

a specific moment in time. But the process of working through all the emotions from the impact of what happened will likely take place over a period of time.

3. *Forgiveness doesn't let the other person off the hook. It actually places them in God's hands.* Forgiving the one who hurt you does not mean you are freeing them from the consequences of their sin. It does mean you refuse the burden of taking revenge and trust God to execute His justice with appropriate measures of mercy.

4. *Forgiveness does not justify or excuse abuse.* While the limitless grace of God provides a way for all to be forgiven, the truth of God provides parameters so that wrong behavior can be addressed. Abuse is not to be tolerated. It is right for you to establish boundaries with equal measures of mercy and tough love.

5. *Forgiveness is required by God, but reconciliation is conditional.* Forgiving someone doesn't mean that trust is immediately restored or that hard relational dynamics are instantly fixed. Reconciliation is dependent on two people being willing to work on the relationship. In some cases, reconciliation is simply not an option. But that doesn't make forgiveness any less healing for you.

6. *Forgiveness isn't an act of our determination. Forgiveness is only made possible by our cooperation.* When I wrongly think my ability to forgive rises and falls on all my efforts—mustered-up grit, conjured maturity, bossed-around resistance, and gentle feelings that feel real one moment and fake the next—I'll never be able to authentically give the kind of forgiveness Jesus has given me. In reality, my ability to forgive others rises and falls on this: leaning into what Jesus has already done, which allows His grace for me to flow freely through me (Ephesians 4:7).

7. *Forgiveness isn't adding on top of our pain a misery too great to bear.* It's exchanging our bound-up resentment for a life-giving freedom, thus making the mystery of the workings of God too great to deny. It is a complicated grace that uncomplicates our blinding pain and helps us see beautiful again.

Please know this isn't a message I've waltzed through writing *or* living.

When your heart has been shattered and reshaped into something that doesn't quite feel normal inside your own chest yet, forgiveness can feel a bit unrealistic.

But here is what I've learned and what I long for you to know too: *forgiveness is possible.* And it is good. Your heart is much too beautiful a place for unhealed pain. Your soul is much too deserving of new possibilities to stay stuck here. And today is the perfect day to start taking steps on this unexpected, miraculous pathway to healing.

Look back at the seven truths I listed above. Which ones resonate the most with your heart?

....
....
....
....
....
....

What are you thankful that forgiveness is *not*? What are you thankful that forgiveness *is*?

....
....
....
....
....
....
....

Have you felt guilty or thought you're not a good Christian because you find forgiveness difficult in some situations? How does it feel to know that you are not alone in this struggle and that forgiveness and healing are processes that take time?

....
....
....
....
....
....
....

Take some time to write out a gut-honest prayer as you begin this journey. Feel free to pour out all your doubts and fears in this prayer. But then invite God to do what only He can do as you surrender your heart to Him through this process.

....

....

....

....

....

....

....

....

....

....

Have hope with me, friend. You and I are in the hands of a compassionate God. Believe with me that He will take care of us and do mighty works in our hearts.

With you on this journey,

* US*

HOW TO USE THIS JOURNAL

THIS JOURNAL IS MEANT to be used side by side with the book. Here I will guide you in digging deeper into what we are reading in each chapter of *Forgiving What You Can't Forget*.

Each chapter of this journal starts with a short reading to connect what you read in the book to what we will be processing in the journal, followed by these four sections:

Keep—quotes from that chapter of *Forgiving What You Can't Forget* that will be good to remember and repeat back to yourself.

Read—key scriptures found in that chapter or that relate to the topics discussed.

Journal—prompts that will help you respond, personally reflect, process, write about, and implement all that we'll be learning.

Pray—short prayers I've typed out to get you started in lifting everything you're working through up to the Lord.

These simple sections will help you work toward applying and living out the message of *Forgiving What You Can't Forget*.

This forgiveness message is not one to just read and then set aside, but one we will want to sit with and return to for years to come. This is where we're learning what to do with our pain and how to walk with God in the midst of it—how to root out our unresolved hurt and keep our hearts open so that healing and peace can come in. Here we are inviting God to turn our pain into a doorway of discovery and learning how to make compassion and forgiveness our way of life.

I Still Cry Over What Happened

I THINK WE ALL have things about our lives that we feel we can count on no matter what. My marriage was one of those things for me. I remember thinking when other hard storms hit me and my family, "At least I know Art and I are good. And as long as we are okay, we can make it through anything together."

And then one day I could no longer use that statement. I discovered that Art had been unfaithful, and all the devastating details that unfolded afterward left me reeling in shock and heartbreak.

It's been a while since "the day everything changed," yet emotions can stir within me that make the pain seem fresh all over again. And tears return.

Maybe you can relate. I wish I could hear your story.

Maybe you've been struggling to do normal life with soul-blinding pain and a confusing mix of emotions. I understand. Maybe you feel lost in your own life because the pain has permeated everything, reframing your entire life story. I get that too.

It feels like there was an enormous earthquake, and now we're trying to find our footing on unstable ground with wide cracks and gaping holes. Yet we're supposed to act like it's all fine. The thought of being trapped here is terrifying, and there's no running away because the pain is inside of us

This is how it feels. But the reality is we don't have to be stuck here.

If we want something different, we can try to do something different. The very idea of that shines a bit of light and hope into our souls.

For now, we will just hold on to two truths: all is not lost, and while the pain can certainly refine us, it does not have to define us (from here on out).

KEEP

Staying here, blaming them, and forever defining your life by what they did will only increase the pain.

———

The more our pain consumes us, the more it will control us.

———

What if it's possible to both let go of what we must but still carry with us what is beautiful and meaningful and true to us?

———

It is necessary for you to not let pain rewrite your memories. And it's absolutely necessary to not let pain ruin your future.

Write any other sentences that personally spoke to you from the introduction of *Forgiving What You Can't Forget*:

....

....

....

....

....

The LORD is my light and my salvation—whom shall I fear? The LORD is the stronghold of my life—of whom shall I be afraid? . . . Your face, LORD, I will seek. . . . Though my father and mother forsake me, the LORD will receive me.

—PSALM 27:1–2, 8, 10

As the deer longs for streams of water, so I long for you, O God. . . . Day and night I have only tears for food. . . . [I'm] praying to God who gives me life. . . . Why am I discouraged? Why is my heart so sad? I will put my hope in God!

—PSALM 42:1, 3, 8, 11 NLT

God is our refuge and strength, an ever-present help in trouble. Therefore we will not fear, though the earth give way and the mountains fall into the heart of the sea. . . . The LORD Almighty is with us; the God of Jacob is our fortress.

—PSALM 46:1–2, 7

What is the defining moment in your life dividing the before and
after of the deep hurt? If you can't think of one defining moment,
what are some other painful experiences you've had that could be
accumulating hurt?

....

....

....

....

....

....

....

The painful event in your life has the potential to darken all of
your memories related to it. But it doesn't have to. In reality, your
memories are a mix of delightful and awful, and you get to choose
what you do with them. Beautiful or painful, they are all your
own authentic experiences.

   Can you see any ways that your pain could be "rewriting
your memories"? Which ones do you want to reclaim as real and
beautiful and completely worth treasuring?

....

....

....

....

....

....

....

How might it look for you to move on without letting go of what is meaningful and true to you?

....

....

....

....

....

When you read the statement "You get to decide how you'll move forward," how does that open up possibilities in your mind for the future? How would you like to move forward?

....

....

....

....

....

PRAY

Father, help me believe that change is possible. Give me hope about the future, not because of how I feel or because of any sign of change, but because You are good. Inspire my imagination as I think about moving forward. You are my Rescuer and my Healer, and my faith is in You. I believe You can restore my heart and redeem the broken parts of my life. In Jesus' name, amen.

CHAPTER 1

FORGIVENESS, THE DOUBLE-EDGED WORD

FORGIVENESS FELT LIKE SOMETHING I might consider far into the future.

Yes, I knew I needed to forgive, but I just *wasn't there yet*. I couldn't imagine ever recovering from the discovery of my husband's affair. The devastation from the relationship implosion impacted every area of my life—my kids, my health, my finances.

Forgiveness? No. Not for a long while. The pain was too overwhelming, the injustice too outrageous, the distrust and resentment in my heart too severe. My life had shattered to pieces after a devastating betrayal . . . how else was I supposed to feel?!

Do you feel it too?

After the blur and shock of the first months, I was still struggling to cope with harsh realities. I was dealing with anxiety and panic attacks. Bitterness and cynicism had set in, and they seemed to hold me together and rip me apart simultaneously.

A heaviness I couldn't shake was always there.

Alone in my darkened world, my feelings kept telling me forgiveness wasn't possible. Forgiveness seemed to hinge on me starting to feel differently or getting my act together. And neither of those were on the horizon.

All the while, God knew I couldn't do it on my own. He actually had something much better ready for me.

You may be right in the thick of that heavy soul feeling right now. I'm so sorry if you are.

Just consider with me right now whether you're thinking of forgiveness wrongly, like I was. It's not something we can muster up on our own. It's all about leaning into what Jesus has already done, which allows His grace *for us* to flow freely *through us*.

And maybe you'll discover what I did. That what our beat-up, bitter, and fearful hearts have been starving for most are the life-giving nourishment of receiving grace and the life-saving satisfaction of giving grace.

STUDIES SHOW THAT CONTINUALLY REVISITING
HURTFUL MEMORIES AND HOLDING A GRUDGE
WORSEN A PERSON'S HEALTH, WHILE GRANTING
FORGIVENESS IMPROVES IT. EVEN IMAGINING THE
ACT OF FORGIVING AND CULTIVATING EMPATHY
BRINGS EMOTIONAL AND PHYSIOLOGICAL BENEFITS.[1]

KEEP

Forgiveness isn't something hard we have the option
to do or not to do. Forgiveness is something hard-
won we have the opportunity to participate in.

———

Forgiveness isn't an act of my determination.
Forgiveness is only made possible by my cooperation.

———

God can redeem your life, even if damaged
human relationships don't come back together.

———

The scenery for your life should not be the pit of
pain that person dragged you down into. There's so
much more to see and discover and experience.

———

Those who cooperate most fully with
forgiveness are those who dance most
freely in the beauty of redemption.

Forgiveness is
the giving, and
so the receiving,
of life.

—GEORGE MACDONALD

Write any other sentences that personally spoke to you from chapter 1 of *Forgiving What You Can't Forget*:

....

....

....

....

....

....

....

....

READ

Even when I walk through the darkest valley,
I will not be afraid, for you are close beside
me. . . . Surely your goodness and unfailing
love will pursue me all the days of my life.

—PSALM 23:4, 6 NLT

He lifted me out of the slimy pit, out of the mud and
mire; he set my feet on a rock and gave me a firm
place to stand. . . . May your love and faithfulness
always protect me. . . . I am poor and needy. . . .
[Lord,] you are my help and my deliverer.

—PSALM 40:2, 11, 17

"You will know the truth, and the
truth will set you free."
—JOHN 8:32

To each one of us grace has been
given as Christ apportioned it.
—EPHESIANS 4:7

A Note from Lysa

"You prepare a table before me . . . [and] anoint my head
with oil; my cup overflows," reads Psalm 23. "Surely your
goodness and love will follow me all the days of my life"
(vv. 5–6).

We are in relationship with a pursuing God who has a
relentless love.

This is the love that seeks out the one lost sheep.
This is the love that fights to rescue His people, Israel,
out of slavery and pursues them with mercy when they
rebel. Moved by compassion, He said, "I will heal their
waywardness and love them freely" (Hosea 14:4).

This is the love that sent His Son to die to save His
treasured people, the love that overpowers everything else.

Here we are with our sorrow and fear, our sin and
resentments overwhelming us. And He has come running.
He stands at the top of the pit we're stuck in, reaching
down to pull us up into the orbit of His all-conquering love.

He wants us to grab hold of Him so He can do in our
lives what only He can do.

JOURNAL

Is there any part of you that is stuck living in unforgiveness? How are you experiencing the effects of that?

....
....
....
....
....
....
....
....

Pursuing forgiveness involves the decision to take away the power from the people who hurt you. How would things change for you if you no longer felt like they had that power?

....
....
....
....
....
....
....
....

God offers you an exchange: release your demand for the people who hurt you to repent, pay you back, be reprimanded, or suffer like you have, and you'll receive the freedom to move on. How does that sound to you today? What does it make you think and feel?

....

....

....

....

....

....

....

....

In this chapter of *Forgiving What You Can't Forget*, we read, "Forgiveness isn't always about doing something for a human relationship but rather being obedient to what God has instructed us to do." In what way does this idea affect your thinking about forgiveness?

....

....

....

....

....

....

....

....

This one is a tough one, and it's okay to come back to it later or skip it if you're not ready.

Reread these statements: "My first inclination most of the time isn't to bless those who hurt me. . . . My first inclination is to do the very thing I'm so critical of them doing. . . . And when sin is my choice, the cover of darkness is my preference."

I am not bringing this up to stir up more hardship or pain for you. I can name many ways I have done this, and I know how hard it is to admit. How have you seen yourself doing this too? What do you see resulting from it?

....

....

....

....

....

....

....

God invites you to *join Him* in His work of forgiveness. He wants to bring it into your life and to the people around you. He's not asking you to muscle your way to "being nice," or pretend things are fine, or even tidy up your internal mess. He's asking for your willingness to depend on His strength for every part of it.

He's offering you forgiveness and a way for you to offer that forgiveness to others. *He is the source for both.*

You can move in this direction without fully understanding it. And you can do it while you're feeling everything you're feeling right now. Emotional healing is a separate issue that will take time. For now, you just need to grab God's hand. Let Him pull you out of that pit of pain, free you from unforgiveness, and lead you in the way of healing from here.

Forgiveness is one of our best weapons against the enemy. How does that speak to you, and what do you think it means?

....
....
....
....
....
....
....
....

How could the experience of forgiveness be good for your heart in this season?

....
....
....
....

How can you begin to cooperate with God in this process of forgiveness?

....
....
....
....

Give yourself time to sit with your difficult emotions—not to wallow in them but to fully acknowledge them. It's important to do this before you rush past them to the next step. What might that look like for you?

_____

_____

_____

_____

_____

_____

_____

PRAY

Father, I want to be a person who walks in the freedom of forgiveness with no hinderance or weight holding me down. I've got questions, some lingering confusion, and hurts that are stacked up in my life. Will You open my mind and heart as I read, and show me the truth You offer me in Your Word as I move toward forgiveness? Thank You for caring about my heart and having such compassion for the pain I've experienced. Knowing You only have my best interest in mind helps me believe forgiveness is possible. In Jesus' name, amen.

CHAPTER 2

WELCOME TO THE TABLE

I'M HERE AT THE GRAY wooden table again, along with some friends just like you. Fellow vulnerable human beings with stacked-up hurts, each on their own forgiveness journeys. This is where we come and sit with our brokenness and confusion. This is where we share our questioning and wrestling.

I'm so glad you're here too.

There's no judging, no bossing, no shaming. We are where we are. We tenderly hold each other's heartbreak and respect each other's need for truth.

This sense of togetherness helps us keep our hearts open to God's message about forgiveness. Our natural inclination is to resist it altogether. And honestly, we're not totally clear about *how* to forgive and what it looks like in real life. Our hearts feel yanked from one difficult experience to the next. Our hurt feelings have left us in a fog that takes over our perspective.

Friend, this is exactly when we need God's Word to show us forgiveness with skin on. To show us Jesus coming for us with forgiveness pulsing through the blood He shed for us. To tell us forgiveness *isn't* impossible when we've been so very forgiven by God Himself. To not run away from forgiveness because we think it'll add more misery to our pain. In reality, it will lead us to healing.

Here, with our hearts open to God's message of forgiveness, we also need to be open about what might be holding us back from this healing. Our coping mechanisms have allowed us to function in everyday life, but they've become barriers to what we need to address and work through.

Again, remember where you are . . . at the gray table, in the company of fellow strugglers. Our honesty in this safe place is setting us on the path to receiving the life-giving freedom God has for us.

KEEP

Forgiveness is a command. But it is not cruel.
It is God's divine mercy for human hearts
that are so prone to turn hurt into hate.

———

We can only heal what we're willing
to acknowledge is real.

———

Unhealed hurt often becomes unleashed
hurt spewed out on others.

———

In the split second of that first utterance
of forgiveness, evil is arrested, heaven
touches earth, and the richest evidence of
the truth of the gospel reverberates not just
that day but for generations to come.

———

While salvation is what brings the flesh of
a human into perfect alignment with the
Spirit of God, forgiveness is the greatest
evidence that the Truth of God lives in us.

Write any other sentences that personally spoke to you from chapter 2 of *Forgiving What You Can't Forget*:

I call on you, my God, for you will answer me;
turn your ear to me and hear my prayer.
Show me the wonders of your great love, you who save
by your right hand those who take refuge in you. . . .
Keep me as the apple of your eye; hide me in the
shadow of your wings.

—PSALM 17:6–8

The LORD, my God, lights up my darkness.

—PSALM 18:28 NLT

Your word is a lamp for my feet, a light on my path.

—PSALM 119:105

"I will forgive their wickedness and will
remember their sins no more."

—HEBREWS 8:12

Now that you know the Bible doesn't demand that we "forgive and forget," write any misconceptions you had around this statement.

How does it help you to know that some things we need to forgive are probably not going to be things we forget, at least not right away? But, simultaneously, we do need to let go of some parts of our past. How do we do this?

Look back at what you wrote in the "Working Through Forgiveness Together" section about your feelings of resistance, confusion, or fear you have toward forgiveness. In all the research I've done on forgiveness, I've found many feelings feeding the resistance that holds many of us back. Circle which of these resonates with you:

- I fear the offense will be repeated.
- Hanging on to a grudge gives me a sense of control in a situation that's felt so unfair.
- The pain I experienced altered my life, and yet no one has ever validated that what I went through was wrong.
- Forgiveness feels like it trivializes, minimizes, or, worse yet, makes what happened no big deal.
- I can't possibly forgive when I still feel so hostile toward the one who hurt me.
- I'm not ready to forgive.
- I still feel hurt.
- They haven't apologized or even acknowledged that what they did was wrong.
- Being back in relationship with this person isn't possible or safe. Furthermore, it's not even reasonable for me to have a conversation with the person who hurt me.
- I'm still in the middle of a long, hard situation with no resolution yet.
- I'm afraid forgiveness will give them false hope that I want to reestablish the relationship, but I don't.
- It's easier to ignore this person altogether than to try and figure out boundaries so they don't keep hurting me.

- What they did is unchangeable; therefore, forgiveness won't help anything.
- The person who hurt me is no longer here. I can't forgive someone I can't talk to.
- I don't think any good will come from forgiveness now.

When I was going through my marriage devastation, I kept telling my counselor I was resisting forgiveness because I needed to know how my story was going to turn out before I could really forgive. Would Art and I wind up together or not? This question haunted me because I didn't want to attach my healing to us reconciling and then get hurt all over again if that didn't happen.

Have you found the fear of the unknown outcome in your situation holding you back from forgiving? How so?

....

....

....

....

....

....

....

Here are two quotes that are worth processing a little more:

- "At some point we must stop imagining the way things should be so much that we can't acknowledge what is."
- "You can only heal what you're willing to acknowledge is real."

Is there anything you've been denying or trying to avoid so you don't have to acknowledge reality? Is there any situation where you are living what you wish were true rather than what is actually true? Write your thoughts below.

....

....

....

....

....

....

Denying and avoiding our pain aren't the only ways we hold ourselves back from forgiving. Other times we get stuck in our pain because we're using coping mechanisms to numb it. My counselor helped me see what I was using as a coping mechanism. I was trying to spin everything in a more positive or hyperspiritual light so I could give the appearance of being more okay than I actually was.

Underline one of these statements that you've caught yourself using to gloss over your pain:

- I'm good. I'm fine. I've just decided to move on.
- Their loss for walking away from me.
- God will eventually make everything all right.
- As a Christian, I know I should forgive, so I have.
- What's in the past is in the past. I'm just walking forward. No big deal.
- There's so much to be thankful for, so I'm just choosing to be grateful.

- Who has the time or energy to unpack why this happened and how it affected me? Let's just move on.
- I'm mature enough to say, "It is what it is," and get over it.

Describe in more detail how this has played out for you.

....

....

....

....

....

....

....

....

It seems an awful lot easier to deny your pain than to do the hard work of dealing with it and healing what's really there. Here are some different examples of coping mechanisms:

- Escaping through bingeing movies, TV shows, or romantic novels, or always finding a new hobby to devote your attention to
- Staying constantly busy, overworking, or oversocializing
- Withdrawing through excessive napping, mindlessly scrolling through social media, or daydreaming
- Numbing out through binge eating, excessive spending, drinking, or using other substances

Now try to be completely honest with yourself. Which of these coping mechanisms, or others that you can think of, do you find yourself doing? Simply acknowledging what or who you are relying on to numb your pain is a gigantic leap forward.

Who can you talk to about this to start finding the help you may need to navigate healthier choices from here?

What action step can you take this week to make healthier choices?

Keeping the goal of forgiveness in mind will help us continue our efforts. When someone, by the power of God's Spirit, forgives another person, they're going against the natural operations of the world and resisting human inclinations. When have you witnessed this, and how did it affect you?

....

....

....

....

....

A Note from Lysa

Consider replacing any of your unhealthy coping mechanisms with one or more of the following of activities below.

- Allow yourself to cry.
- Do calming breathing exercises while walking outside.
- Write about your feelings.
- Decide on a way to describe how you're really doing so you can be authentic when people ask. For example, "Honestly, it's really hard right now. I'm taking it one day at a time."
- Create a guiding phrase that you can return to daily. For example, "This is not forever," "Just do right now," or "God's power will do what I cannot."
- Pray and spend time listening for God's comfort or challenge to you.
- Read Scripture.

- Talk with a friend about your feelings.
- List good things about your present reality.
- Read books written by those who have gone through similar pain and glean from their helpful perspectives and experiential wisdom.
- Go to a counselor who specializes in helping heal others with your same struggle, or go to a support group specific to your needs.

Here are more healthy activities to do *in moderation*. We're not trying to escape reality. We're trying to take care of ourselves by doing a variety of things that nourish, energize, and calm us so we have the strength to process our pain.

- Exercise and stretch.
- Take a hot shower or bath.
- Spend time outdoors in the beauty of nature.
- Listen to music.
- Do something that makes you laugh.
- Read a book that either gives your brain a break or stimulates it in a healthy way.
- Play with a pet.
- Socialize with friends.
- Diffuse a smell you like (mine is lemon and lavender).
- Play a game.
- Work on a puzzle.
- Be creative somehow—cook, draw, garden, etc.
- Do something helpful for someone else.
- Do something that makes you feel connected to memories you love.
- Do something that makes you feel like you again.
- Create simple routines involving healthy activities to help you build a sense of stability in this season.

Father, I want to fully cooperate with You. Show me the parts of my life, especially in the area of resistance to forgiveness and unhealthy coping mechanisms, where I need to lean in to You and to those who want to help me. I don't want to avoid, deny, or hide anymore. I want to heal all areas of unresolved hurt and pain in my heart. You are good and faithful, and I trust You as You lead me in this. In Jesus' name, amen.

CHAPTER 3

IS THIS EVEN SURVIVABLE?

IF I WERE FORTUNATE enough to meet you today, I would be fascinated to learn many details of your life and what makes you, you. And then I'd share what makes me, me. And I imagine that while we'd have experiences that make us different, one part of us would be very much the same. We've both been hurt.

And in that reality of shed tears, we'd find we are so very much alike.

I understand what it feels like to walk around with deep wounds that sometimes trigger all-consuming emotions. We have exhausted every effort imaginable to manage our feelings, but we aren't sure if it's possible to truly find healing.

But when we hear the word *forgiveness*, we shrink back. That seems like a step to consider much later when we've healed and after we are certain the one who hurt us is truly sorry for what they did. No, we're not ready to sign up for forgiveness.

I understand.

So that's why we aren't starting with forgiving the one or ones who hurt us the most. Not yet. We have to start by being willing to consider removing the unfair hold our pain has on us.

Then we can stop fixating on the ones who hurt us and start focusing on what will heal us.

So how do we do this? By realizing that waiting on others to right their wrongs paralyzes our own progress. Our pain and our feelings are *ours* to manage, no one else's. We are impacted by the actions and words of others, but we shouldn't give them the power to dictate our emotions. We can't control the actions of others, but we can control our reactions. We can be hurt without turning into a person who lives hurt.

Instead of just letting what we feel in any given moment run wild, yanking our mood up and down, we can better confront and stabilize our feelings with healthy perspectives. If we wanted to tame a wild horse, we wouldn't ignore it or indulge it. We'd have to be brave and confront its need to be harnessed.

This forward movement helps us turn toward the possibility of hope.

We're setting out to free ourselves from grim, hopeless pursuits that leave us stuck in anger and void of peace. We're opening ourselves up to the glorious, hope-filled possibilities of the future. And we can begin to see a glimmer of the reality that healing can happen.

God of our life, there are days when the burdens we carry chafe our shoulders and weigh us down; when the road seems *dreary and endless,* the skies grey and threatening; when our lives have no music in them, our *hearts are lonely,* and our souls have lost their courage. *Flood the path* with light. Turn our eyes to where the skies are full of promise; tune our hearts to *brave music.*

—AUGUSTINE

KEEP

Forgiveness is a complicated grace that
uncomplicates my blinding pain and
helps me see beautiful again.

———

Unresolved pain triggers unrestrained chaos.

———

If healing hasn't been worked out and
forgiveness hasn't been walked out, chaos
is what will continue to play out.

———

That person who hurt me may be the cause of
the pain. But they are not capable of being the
healer of my pain or the restorer of my life.

———

Blame hands the power to change over
to the person who hurt me.

———

What we look for is what we will see. What
we see determines our perspective. And
our perspective becomes our reality.

Write any other sentences that spoke to you from chapter 3 of
Forgiving What You Can't Forget:

....

....

....

....

....

....

The LORD is close to the brokenhearted and
saves those who are crushed in spirit.

—PSALM 34:18

I am exhausted and completed crushed. My
groans come from an anguished heart. You know
what I long for, Lord; you hear my every sigh.

—PSALM 38:8–9 NLT

Like a city whose walls are broken through
is a person who lacks self-control.

—PROVERBS 25:28

The fruit of the Spirit is love, joy,
peace, patience, kindness, goodness,
faithfulness, gentleness, self-control.

—GALATIANS 5:22–23 ESV

The Spirit God gave us does not make us timid,
but gives us power, love and self-discipline.

—2 TIMOTHY 1:7

God has said, "Never will I leave you; never will I forsake you." So we say with confidence, "The Lord is my helper."

—HEBREWS 13:5-6

Give all your worries and cares to God, for he cares about you.

—1 PETER 5:7 NLT

A Note from Lysa

Hannah was miserable with grief and sorrow. After spending years longing for a child and enduring ridicule from her husband's other wife, Peninnah (who had many children), she finally hit a breaking point. The pain, and all the emotions that went along with it, took over.

Instead of denying, avoiding, or numbing her pain, Hannah did something brave. She let herself feel that pain and came to God with it. First Samuel 1:10 says, "In her deep anguish Hannah prayed to the LORD, weeping bitterly." She later explained to the priest Eli, who thought she looked so upset she must be drunk, "I was pouring out my soul to the LORD" (v. 15).

Trusting God's love for her meant that Hannah could press in to Him and—with raw soul, honesty, and sob-filled questions—lay everything out before Him. God later answered her prayer to become a mother, but long before that change of circumstances, Hannah knew intimacy with the one who loved her best.

Our God can—and wants to—handle our intense emotions, our mess, our unmet longings, our confusion. He knows our hearts better than we do, yet promises never to leave us.

"Forgiveness is a complicated grace." What do these words mean to you?

If no one else has ever said this to you, I want to: I'm so sorry for what you've been through. Your hurt matters.

And not only do I care about you, but so does God. He sees you. He loves you deeply.

He hurts with you. He wants to shelter you and be your sturdy refuge where you can be real, be raw, be held . . . just *be*. He's ready to wrap you up and keep you close to His heart as you're feeling gutted, broken, and a whole battery of overwhelming emotions. Invite Him in, and He will meet you where you are.

I want you to take comfort in knowing that you will not always feel the way you do today and that you belong to the God who makes healing possible. He is greater than what you are feeling. Even though it feels impossible, He will make a way for you to move forward, carving out a path for you and gently helping you take each step.

God offers you a safe place to process your heartache. I know facing your pain is hard, but honestly acknowledging it is the first step to healing. Ignoring it will just delay change. The only way out is *through*.

While we don't want to go to the other extreme and continually dwell on our pain (that will just get us stuck there), we do need to understand it. Finding words to express it is part of the healthy process of managing it and moving beyond it.

Give yourself the freedom to go ahead and say whatever you are feeling—no judgment. Feelings come and go; they are not who you are.

Write about the hurts you find yourself thinking of and revisiting often by finishing these statements of loss below. Unfiltered is okay.

They took _____ .

He or she didn't even _____ .

I'm afraid I'll never again _____ .

I feel like they got away with _____ .

Why do I still _____ ?

How can I move on from _____ ?

The part that feels impossible is _____ .

I feel I can't _____ .

And the worst part was _____ .

Journal any other thoughts about your hurts here:

....

....

....

....

....

....

Whether or not you realize it, writing all of this out has helped you accept where you are and opened the door to progress.

Next, you need to acknowledge these realities:

- The hurt was caused by someone else, but the resulting feelings are mine to manage.
- If I think I need another person to make things right before I can move toward change, I will forever be exerting my efforts in the wrong direction. I will forever be paralyzed in my progress.
- My job isn't to control anyone else. My job is to manage myself.

Pick two of the following prompts, then journal how you are going to make progress with this and move forward:

I can't manage feelings I don't own.

I can't wait for another person to do something to make me feel better about the situation.

I can't expect other people to manage my feelings for me.

I can't control what I feel, but I can control how I respond to it.

....

....

....

....

....

....

....

....

In this chapter of *Forgiving What You Can't Forget*, you and I said, "Today is my day to stop the grim, hopeless pursuit of expecting the other person to make this right, so that I can receive the glorious, hope-filled possibilities of this new day." What exactly do you think you need to stop expecting from other people?

....

....

....

....

....

....

....

....

Can you imagine, once your focus is truly shifted away from those expectations, how it could open up bright possibilities for your future? What comes to mind?

PRAY

Father, forgiving the pain others have inflicted can seem cruel—even impossible. I am thankful You've given Jesus to us as an example of the ultimate forgiver. Help me love and forgive like Jesus while acknowledging my pain and owning my feelings. I want to live from a place of hope and see beautiful again. In Jesus' name, amen.

*It is easier
to forgive an
enemy than to
forgive a friend.*

—WILLIAM BLAKE

CHAPTER 4

HOW IS FORGIVENESS EVEN POSSIBLE WHEN I FEEL LIKE THIS?

DO I WANT TO HEAL?

Yes. Of course I do.

I know you do too.

We want to become whole and healthy. We want to work through whatever we need to in order to get there. We want to stop hurting and be free of the pain that relentlessly haunts our hearts and hijacks our happiness.

We've taken huge strides toward that by being honest with ourselves about how we cope and by acknowledging how we feel. But right now we still feel like a wreck. Everything in our world seems outrageously unresolved and upside down. We're all wrapped up in a wild tangle of wounds and emotions and wants, and somewhere in there is our desire for change and healing.

So you and I need to separate our healing from everything else—from wanting to have wrongs made right and to have our situation feel fair.

We need to separate our choice to heal from the choices of those who hurt us. If we can just shift our gaze away from the other characters in our story, we can focus on what only we can do. And what only Jesus can do.

Healing is something we choose, and we choose it by obeying.

That's why we need to ask Jesus for His help in this process.

We can tell Him how hard this is. We can tell Him how much this hurts. And He understands in such a deeply personal way. But hard and holy can hold hands. We can take this next step. We can make progress today and bring all our hurt and pain under the power of Jesus' blood, shed for our forgiveness.

KEEP

My ability to heal cannot be conditional on the other person receiving adequate consequences for their disobedience but only on my obedience to trust God's justice whether I ever see it or not.

———

Refusing to forgive is refusing the peace of God.

———

You make the decision to forgive the facts of what happened. But then you must also walk through the process of forgiveness for the impact those facts have had on you.

———

Whatever my feelings don't yet allow for, the blood of Jesus will surely cover.

———

The hurt they caused was most likely from hurt they carried.

Write any other sentences that personally spoke to you from chapter 4 of *Forgiving What You Can't Forget*:

....

....

....

....

....

....

....

"Come to me, all you who are weary and burdened,
and I will give you rest. Take my yoke upon you
and learn from me, for I am gentle and humble
in heart, and you will find rest for your souls."

—MATTHEW 11:28-29

All of you who were baptized into Christ
have clothed yourselves with Christ.

—GALATIANS 3:27

Your life is now hidden with Christ in God.

—COLOSSIANS 3:3

This world is not our permanent home; we are looking
forward to a home yet to come. Therefore, let us
offer through Jesus a continual sacrifice of praise to
God, proclaiming our allegiance to his name. And
don't forget to do good and to share with those in
need. These are the sacrifices that please God. . . .
Now may the God of peace—who brought up from
the dead our Lord Jesus, the great Shepherd of
the sheep, and ratified an eternal covenant with his
blood—may he equip you with all you need for doing
his will. May he produce in you, through the power of
Jesus Christ, every good thing that is pleasing to him.

—HEBREWS 13:14-16, 20-21 NLT

A Note from Lysa

Providing life and wholeness is part of who God is. One of His names, Yahweh-Rapha, even means "the God who heals." Restoration and peace are His will for us.

Yet He calls us to participate in His acts of healing—to express our faith in His power and to embrace the change His healing will bring.

Listen to these words Jesus spoke before and after He healed people:

- "Do you believe that I am able to do this?" (Matthew 9:28).
- "Don't be afraid; just believe, and she will be healed" (Luke 8:50).
- "Do you want to get well? . . . Get up! Pick up your mat and walk" (John 5:6, 8).
- His disciples asked, "Who sinned, this man or his parents, that he was born blind?" Jesus answered, "Neither this man nor his parents sinned . . . but this happened so that the works of God might be displayed in him" (John 9:2–3).

Jesus will draw our focus away from feeling pitiful or pointing fingers and remind us that change is possible. He'll prompt us to zero in on *Him* and to trust His power—to courageously open our arms wide to receive and step into what He wants to accomplish in our lives.

If we choose to do those things, we're taking the path that leads to these sweet words of freedom: "Daughter, your faith has healed you. Go in peace and be freed from your suffering" (Mark 5:34).

Have you ever asked this question: "How could I possibly start healing when there was no resolution or restitution or reconciliation with the ones who hurt me?" What are you learning that is helping you realize no matter what the other person does, you aren't held back from moving forward in healthy, healing ways?

....

....

....

....

....

....

We learned in this chapter of *Forgiving What You Can't Forget* that forgiveness is both a decision and a process. We must first forgive what happened in a marked moment of forgiveness. Then when we are triggered with lingering pain or hard memories after our decision to forgive, we have an opportunity to continue the process of forgiveness by forgiving the impact their actions are still having on us.

Spend some time writing out some of the facts of how you were hurt, who was involved, and the impact this is still having on you, just like I did in my counselor's office, using the instructions below.

- Write each fact you need to forgive on a 3x5 card:
    Person: The name of the person who hurt you.
    Fact: This is what happened and what I need to forgive.
    Impact: This is how this still affects me—how I get triggered and my pain feels fresh all over again.

- Place the cards face up on the table or floor.
- Declare your forgiveness by placing red felt squares over each card. Make sure each felt square is large enough to cover the card entirely.
- As you do so, say, "I forgive _____ for _____. And whatever my feelings don't yet allow for, the blood of Jesus will surely cover."
- Repeat this exercise until you are done interacting with each card.

It wasn't until after I verbalized all my pain like this that I realized what it meant to cooperate with Jesus' forgiveness. It's not about "feeling" my way to forgiveness but rather bringing my *willingness* to forgive and putting my faith in what the cross of Jesus can cover. And it's about seeing myself—and anyone who has hurt me—as Jesus does: broken but still chosen and worth forgiveness.

How might it help you to see those who have hurt you as Jesus sees them—broken but still chosen and worth forgiveness?

If this question is too painful for you to process, try instead to consider one thought of compassion for the hurt your offender must have experienced in order to get to the place where they hurt you. I know this can be a hard processing activity. But it is helpful to have compassion for their pain and unresolved issues, even if you aren't yet ready to have compassion on them. Journal your thoughts here.

A Note from Lysa

Studies have shown that people who forgive others feel less burdened and perceive challenges to be less difficult. One study even found that the act of forgiveness made people feel physically lighter—those who forgave literally jumped higher than those who didn't. Researchers concluded that offering forgiveness unburdens us both mentally and physically, helping us "overcome the negative effects of conflict."[1]

PRAY

Father, I confess I haven't taken the command to forgive seriously because I've always thought my circumstances were unique and my abilities to heal were dependent on resolution, restitution, and reconciliation. Forgive me, Lord, and teach me how to forgive like You have forgiven me and those I'm needing to forgive. In Jesus' name, amen.

Of all the knowledge that we can ever obtain, the knowledge of God, and the knowledge of ourselves, are the most important.

—JONATHAN EDWARDS

CHAPTER 5

COLLECTING THE DOTS

SCARS TELL A STORY of the past. When a wound becomes a scar, it's hard to forget what happened.

I have a large scar that runs up almost the entire length of my torso. I have many scars from breast cancer surgeries. I have a small scar on my face from one of my children, as a toddler, biting me. Each scar has a story.

Can you share about one of your scars? How did you get it, and do you feel it's healed or is in the process of healing?

But when the wound never heals, it's hard to remember you were ever whole. Unhealed wounds not only scream with very present pain but also run the risk of letting infection into the rest of the body. The same is true with emotional wounds.

It's awful when anyone suffers. But the greater tragedy is when their past suffering becomes an inescapable mindset that limits, or even cripples, them for years.

I know all about screaming, unhealed wounds and imprisoning mindsets.

It breaks my heart to think you might too.

Everyone has unresolved pain to some extent, whatever their stories are. But we typically aren't aware just how much that unresolved pain is at the root of many of our struggles.

To deal with that unresolved pain, we have to understand how it got there and how we responded to it. And to do that, we have to understand our own stories. We have to look again at those past events that created the beliefs and scripts we use now.

It's the furthest thing from easy. I know. But waving it off with a "No thanks!" will only keep us right where we are, in the thick of our struggles.

So, with a squeeze of your hand and a spirit of compassion and resolve, I'm leaning into this with you. Let's revisit your story together.

Forgiveness isn't just about what's in front of us. Sometimes a bigger part of the journey is uncovering what is informing us from long ago.

We all have a story. And then we all
have a story we tell ourselves.

———

The greatest hell a human can experience here on
earth is not suffering. It's feeling like the suffering
is pointless and will never get any better.

———

Woven throughout our narratives is a belief
system that formed inside of us as children.

———

We write scripts to help us navigate life experiences
based on our past experiences. And those scripts
turn into belief systems that inform our actions.

Write any other sentences that spoke to you from chapter 5 of
Forgiving What You Can't Forget:

....

....

....

....

....

....

....

....

....

....

....

....

Lord, you have examined me. You know all about me.... You know my thoughts before I think them.... You know well everything I do.... You are all around me—in front and in back. You have put your hand on me.... You made my whole being. You formed me in my mother's body. I praise you because you made me in an amazing and wonderful way.... All the days planned for me were written in your book before I was one day old.

—PSALM 139:1-3, 5, 13-14, 16 ICB

The accuser of our brothers and sisters, who accuses them before our God day and night, has been hurled down. They triumphed over him by the blood of the Lamb and by the word of their testimony.

—REVELATION 12:10-11

Why is the "word of our testimony" or sharing our story of God's redemption so important?

A Note from Lysa

Researchers have found a helpful strategy for reducing the emotional impact of revisiting a negative experience. Instead of focusing on how you felt during the experience, focus on neutral aspects of the context—like the smell in the air, what you were wearing, or a family member who was there.[1]

This insight can help us as we approach the daunting task of remembering our past. While we do want to address the difficult emotions associated with our memories, we don't have to start there. We can begin with the basic facts and non-emotionally charged details. Then slowly move on from there.

There is no need to rush this. Be gentle with yourself and take the time you need.

Let God have your life; He can do more with it than you can.

—D. L. MOODY

JOURNAL

Art and I have shared our story of the devastation that happened in our marriage when he was unfaithful. That story is still so hard for me because even though we've experienced so much healing, it still has pain attached to it. The same is true with my dad abandoning our family. And the man who abused me as a child.

What are some memories from your past that understandably still have strong feelings attached to them?

....

....

....

....

....

....

In the lines below, we're going to divide up your journaled answers for this question into nine categories and focus on both the most beautiful and most difficult memories.

Let your memories leak out onto paper. Don't worry about how the words come out. Don't get tangled up in any sort of time line or ensuring every detail is precise and correct. It's not about getting it all right but rather getting it all out.

Record your memories on the lines that follow. Don't feel like you have to fill in every blank—these are just time-period prompts to help you get started. In the coming chapters, we'll process what to do with these.

EARLIEST MEMORY

BEAUTIFUL: ....

....

....

....

....

....

....

DIFFICULT: ....

....

....

....

....

....

....

CHILDHOOD

BEAUTIFUL: ....

....

....

....

....

....

....

DIFFICULT: ....

....

....

....

....

....

MIDDLE SCHOOL YEARS

BEAUTIFUL: ....

....

....

....

....

....

DIFFICULT: ....

....

....

....

....

....

HIGH SCHOOL YEARS

BEAUTIFUL: ....

....

....

....

....

....

DIFFICULT: ....

....

....

....

....

....

COLLEGE YEARS

BEAUTIFUL: ....

....

....

....

....

....

....

DIFFICULT: ....

....

....

....

....

....

....

YOUNG ADULT YEARS

BEAUTIFUL: ....

....

....

....

....

....

DIFFICULT: ....

....

....

....

....

....

....

MY 30s

BEAUTIFUL: ....

....

....

....

....

....

DIFFICULT: ....

....

....

....

....

....

MY 40s

BEAUTIFUL: ....

....

....

....

....

....

DIFFICULT: ....

....

....

....

....

....

BEYOND

BEAUTIFUL: ....

....

....

....

....

....

....

DIFFICULT: ....

....

....

....

....

....

In this chapter of *Forgiving What You Can't Forget*, I talked about a season of my life when it was just my mom and me trying to process some hard things. I desperately wanted my dad to accept, love, and protect me. This kind of fatherly experience seemed completely out of reach, and I felt like it was somehow my fault. Have you ever wanted something that should have been possible but didn't seem possible for *you*? Write your thoughts below.

Reread this statement: "The greatest hell a human can experience here on earth is not suffering. It's feeling like the suffering is pointless and it will never get any better." What are your thoughts about this in light of doing work to uncover the hard parts of your story?

Father, I don't always tie my current mindsets and struggles back to my earliest days. But doing this is not to revisit the hurt but rather identify places where healing still needs to be worked on. Help me remember and process all that You'd have me recall today. This isn't fun or easy, but I desire to be a person who is whole and full of grace, not only for myself, but for those who have played a part in who I've become, for better or worse. In Jesus' name, amen.

CHAPTER 6

CONNECTING THE DOTS

CAN I OFFER YOU some encouragement from my heart to yours? You are amazing for sticking with this hard work of forgiveness.

You could have given up a while ago. You could have flung this journal across the room as soon as it got too tough.

Well, maybe you did. But you're back. And there's progress worth celebrating.

In the last chapter, you wrote out the significant points of your history, and now we're going to walk back through them. We're going to find the story *behind* your story—to see how your beliefs and behaviors are tied to those experiences.

Now, I am well aware that it will take courage to explore your story and sit with it long enough to understand yourself in it more deeply, and you may not feel ready.

I am very familiar with this feeling.

But keep in mind, this isn't about conjuring up courage we aren't sure we have. This is about leaning into the Lord's strength promised to us. The prophet Habakkuk wrote, "God, the Lord, is my strength; he makes my feet like the deer's; he makes me tread on my high places" (3:19 ESV). When Habakkuk wrote this, God's people were enduring suffering and injustice. But God reminded them that He would make things right and that His power and love were always available to them. He would give them courage and strength. God is the one who gives us steady feet like a deer and the courage to walk with confidence on high places—even near cliffs that would terrify us if not for His assurance.

I'm going to guide you through this process. Once you understand God's truth, you'll be able to bring more of His wisdom into your life. It will also help you identify people who might still need to be forgiven in your story, and help you move forward in healthy ways.

Life can only be understood backwards; but it must be lived forwards.

—SØREN KIERKEGAARD

KEEP

The things marking us from yesterday are
still part of the making of us today.

———

We can't expect another person to carry the
burden of making us feel better about who we are.
They may need to do a better job at loving us . . .
but that's their journey to take if they're willing.

———

Everything lost that we place in the
hands of God isn't a forever loss.

———

We don't want to forever process hard
situations using perceptions formed by our
most hurtful or traumatic seasons.

———

We can't change what we have experienced, but
we can choose how the experiences change us.

Write any other sentences that spoke to you from chapter 6
Forgiving What You Can't Forget:

....

....

....

....

....

....

....

God created mankind in his own image. . . . God
saw all that he had made, and it was very good.
—GENESIS 1:27, 31

Call out for insight and cry aloud for
understanding . . . look for it as for silver
and search for it as for hidden treasure.
—PROVERBS 2:3–4

"Very truly I tell you, unless a kernel of wheat falls
to the ground and dies, it remains only a single
seed. But if it dies, it produces many seeds."
—JOHN 12:24

Accept one another, then, just as Christ accepted you.
—ROMANS 15:7

In this chapter of *Forgiving What You Can't Forget*, I talked about how connecting the dots helped me see some perceptions and behavior patterns in my relationship with Art that needed to change.

We were able to be more authentically vulnerable once we acknowledged we both needed grace and healing. What we've done, while it may be a call to action to get healthy, is not a summation of who we are. In His love the Lord makes us both acceptable and accepted.

These are truths we could begin to live out in our relationship because God had already helped us believe them as individuals first. In moments of vulnerability, we could simply remind each other of what we already knew to be true.

We had to realize that God is in charge of the fixing. And that frees us to just do the living and the loving together.

This highlights an important reality: you and I can't expect another person to carry the burden of making us feel better about who we are, fixing who we are, or completing who we are.

Where might you be expecting others to do these things for you? Also, what complicates this for you? For example, I know my husband can't fix my trust issues. But whether or not I feel safe in our relationship is affected by what he does and doesn't do.

Now that you've collected some of the pieces of your story from the last chapter, it's time to start making some connections to how those experiences shaped you. This includes what you believe about God, yourself, and others, and what you should and should not do. These beliefs have formed your processing system through which you interpret what you're experiencing today.

Let's walk through an activity to help us become more aware of how we might be processing things.

FORGIVENESS: What were you taught as a child about forgiveness?

....
....
....
....
....
....
....

RESENTMENT: What was modeled by your parents and other influential people about how to handle being hurt, holding grudges, and resenting other people?

....
....
....
....
....
....

RETALIATION: What is your first memory of seeing someone retaliate, and how did that affect you?

....
....
....
....
....
....
....
....
....
....

RECONCILIATION: Is there anything from your story that has led you to misunderstand that reconciliation and forgiveness always have to go together? Is there something from your story that makes you believe reconciliation in some relationships isn't healthy or possible?

....
....
....
....
....
....
....
....
....
....

GRACE: How was grace talked about by influential people in your childhood? Was grace modeled in your home?

....
....
....
....
....
....
....
....
....

GOD: Think of a particularly painful event or relationship you're still processing. What are your honest thoughts about why God allowed this pain into your life? Can these thoughts be traced back to a hard experience earlier in life?

....
....
....
....
....
....
....
....
....
....

YOURSELF: What are some beliefs you have about yourself—both positive and negative—based on significant experiences in your younger years? And on more current situations you've walked through?

....
....
....
....
....
....
....
....
....

OTHERS WHO'VE HURT YOU: Consider whether you have a general belief or approach regarding other people in the following areas: Can they be trusted? Are people good or bad? Do people have good intentions or hidden motivations? Are people for you or out to get you? Do you find yourself enjoying people or feeling like you need to constantly manage them? Do you try to avoid others as much as possible? Write down which of these resonates with you and why.

....
....
....
....
....
....
....
....
....

WHAT PEOPLE SHOULD AND SHOULD NOT DO: List some of the most important rules you hold sacred about how you should treat others. Then list your rules for how others should treat you.

Some connections from our past experiences are more subtle and manifest as triggered feelings rather than belief systems. As you've recalled certain people and circumstances from your past, pay attention to physical responses your body has, such as an increased heart rate, anxious feelings, grimacing expressions, or just a general feeling of resistance you know shouldn't be there. What do you notice?

Are there times of the day or seasons of the year that you should enjoy but you find yourself dreading and disliking?

For example, I have always loved October and November. Fall has always been such a special time of the year for me. But now I find myself bracing for these fall months, because it's when a significant trauma happened with Art. Once I made this connection, I intentionally worked to reclaim these months for good. Reclaiming is so much more empowering than avoiding.

....

....

....

....

....

....

Are there places you should enjoy, but you find yourself not wanting to go there?

....

....

....

....

Are there certain personalities or qualities in people you avoid or find yourself feeling especially anxious around?

....

....

....

....

Are there certain words or phrases that trigger more emotion than you feel they should?

Are there life events that when the memories are talked about, you find yourself wanting to escape the conversation?

Now, are there any other significant patterns or connections you've realized as you've taken time to think about how your life experiences have shaped you, grown you, or held you back?

We connect the dots in order to understand ourselves better so we can develop beliefs and processing systems based on truth. This process can unfold for years as we realize how things have affected us. The emotional cost of a painful experience sometimes takes years to fully understand. You have been impacted by what you've experienced. How has the pain you've experienced impacted you, what pain still remains, and what still needs to be forgiven?

....

....

....

....

....

....

....

....

I have a great need for Christ, I have a great Christ for my need.

—CHARLES SPURGEON

PRAY

Father, thank You for leading me to revisit some of my long-held beliefs and perspectives, both healthy and not healthy. Please take my shame and hurt and help me see beautiful again. Continue to help me see who I really am in light of who You are. In Jesus' name, amen.

CHAPTER 7

CORRECTING THE DOTS

I'M STARTING TO SEE another reality in my scars. They don't have to be ugly reminders. Scars are beautiful when we see them as glorious reminders that we courageously survived—when we let them tell the story of our God who fights for us, heals us, and faithfully sees us through.

We've acknowledged the pain in our past and begun to understand its impact. We accept these realities as permanent ink dried on the pages of our story.

And we get to decide what comes next. We choose what we do with what we have and how we see what we've been through.

It's like we're a house in need of renovation. It's full of possibilities, but it'll require some work. And a lot of time. Walls will need to be torn down and rebuilt. The foundation will have to be strengthened.

Our skewed perspectives, beliefs not based on truth, and unhealthy thought and behavior patterns—those all will have to go. In their place we'll need to develop a healthier system of processing all our feelings, perceptions, and decisions.

It'd be so much easier to live in the run-down house as it is. To stick with what's familiar and keep on thinking and living the way we have been. I know. I did that for quite a while. But doing that will keep us trapped, running into the same problems and the same pain.

Remember, we're not left to do this all on our own. God is here and He is at work. He wants to turn our prison of pain into a gateway to growth. He wants to free us from anything holding us back from forgiveness, wholeness, and healthy relationships. He wants to produce new beauty and life in us.

But we've got to say yes to Him. And then dive into the transforming work with Him.

KEEP

The experiences I have affect the perceptions I form. The perceptions I form become the beliefs I carry. The beliefs I carry determine what I see.

———

Forgiveness isn't nearly as hard for me when I have a healthier system of processing my thoughts, my feelings, my perceptions, and beliefs

———

It's impossible to travel through life and not collect emotional souvenirs.

———

I can't always see what's inside my heart, but I can listen to what spills out.

———

There is a healed version of me that is waiting and wanting to emerge.

Write any other sentences that spoke to you from chapter 7 of *Forgiving What You Can't Forget*:

We also glory in our sufferings, because we know that suffering produces perseverance; perseverance, character; and character, hope. And hope does not put us to shame, because God's love has been poured out into our hearts through the Holy Spirit, who has been given to us.

—ROMANS 5:3-5

If any of you lacks wisdom, you should ask God, who gives generously to all without finding fault, and it will be given to you.

—JAMES 1:5

Do not merely listen to the word, and so deceive yourselves. Do what it says.

—JAMES 1:22

If we claim to be without sin, we deceive ourselves and the truth is not in us.

—1 JOHN 1:8

Those who dive in the sea of affliction bring up rare pearls.

—CHARLES SPURGEON

A Note from Lysa

Who are you? What determines your identity? What limits or frees you? What weakens or empowers you?

Henry Nouwen warns us of five lies of identity:

1. I am what I have.
2. I am what I do.
3. I am what other people say or think of me.
4. I am nothing more than my worst moment.
5. I am nothing less than my best moment.[1]

I have a suspicion that Stephen (the first Christian martyr), Saul (who would become Paul), and Peter all faced aspects of these lies about their identity.

Stephen may have been caught in a moment where he knew what he did and how he spoke would be a reflection of his beliefs (I am what I do).

Saul may have been tormented by the fact that he was the instigator and initiator of Stephen's murder (I am nothing more than my worst moment).

Peter may have been horrified by his impulse to compromise for the sake of what others thought of him (I am what other people say or think of me).

However, for each of these five lies there is a brilliant truth.

1. My identity is what I have in Christ—salvation and freedom from sin and death.
2. I don't have to worry about "doing" to prove anything, because Christ has done what needed to be done on the cross.
3. I am what God says of me, and that helps me not fall into

people pleasing and helps me keep what others say about me in perspective.

4. My relationship with God is safe and secure even in the midst of my very worst moments.

5. I rejoice in all that God has done for me in my very best moments.

Which of these five identity lies can you see might be a personal struggle for you? As you identify which of these you resonate with, can you see how something from your past is feeding that perception?

....

....

....

....

....

....

....

....

Which truth do you need most to overcome that lie? Write your thoughts below.

....

....

....

....

....

....

....

....

....

I would suspect some of what has caused you pain has affected how you view your identity. But it doesn't get to dictate what you become.

Once we understand this, we can break free from wrongly believing we are a sum total of what happens to us. We can stop seeing ourselves as the wounded one, the rejected one, the incomplete one, the damaged one.

The truth of God's Word shows us that we are quite the opposite. We are the ones set up for perseverance that produces character and strengthened hope (Romans 5:4). We are the ones set up for great endurance and patience (Colossians 1:11–12). And we are the ones set up to be more mature on the other side of any trial (James 1:2–4).

Once we settle that what has happened to us, when processed through God's truth, doesn't have to alter our lives in only negative ways, we have new room for growth. We are empowered to become who God created us to be—whole and healthy, loved and loving, freed and forgiving.

Did you see yourself in any of the toxic tendencies mentioned in this chapter, like:

- Being quick to perceive the words and actions of others as personal attacks
- Building a case to support your perceptions
- Assigning wrong motives and negative interpretations to what is said and done to you?

If so, write your thoughts below.

....
....
....
....
....
....
....

Are there any other unhealthy relationship tendencies you can see in yourself?

....
....
....
....
....
....
....
....

Are there any dots you've connected or any of your perspectives that have shifted that might help you start processing some of your current relational situations in a healthier way? How so?

....

....

....

....

....

Helen Keller once thanked God for her handicaps because she felt that through them she found herself, her work, and her God. Reflecting on this, I realize some of the hardest things I've walked through helped me recognize my calling and step into the most meaningful work of my life.

After my perspectives started shifting, it was important for me to reconsider perceptions of painful experiences. What had I come to believe was true about every person involved? What story was I telling myself now? What still needed to be corrected so I could have healthier interpretations of what I saw—in my past and present?

For these next questions, think about a specific instance you're facing where processing it using what we've been learning in this book could help you look at some things differently.

What do you now believe about the person who hurt you?

....

....

....

....

....

What do you now believe about other people who witnessed or knew about what happened?

....
....
....
....
....
....

And what do you now believe about God as a result of this whole experience?

....
....
....
....
....
....
....

Is there a redeeming part of this story you can focus on?

....
....
....
....
....
....

What good could come about if you decide to forgive and not keep dwelling on all the ways you were hurt?

....
....
....
....
....
....

Are there positive qualities about yourself that can emerge if you choose to move forward without holding on to grudges?

....
....
....
....
....
....
....

Finally, we want to process our suffering through the fact that God never wastes it. Read Romans 5:3–5 again (find it in the "Read" section). And look again at a statement from chapter 6 of *Forgiving What You Can't Forget*: "Inside every loss, a more wise, empathetic, understanding, discerning, compassionate person of strength and humility has the potential to arise within us."

What would a healthy version of you be empowered to do from here?

How can this hurt make you better, not worse?

What might God be giving or revealing to you through this that you couldn't have received before?

This isn't something you can just whiz through in a couple of hours or even a couple of days.

These revelations may come over time and in unexpected ways. Whenever you are inspired to write down what you're learning, let the words flow. Be honest with what emerges. And keep checking in on the canary in your coal mine by paying attention to writing that starts blaming others or revisiting the circumstances of your pain.

One thing I kept noticing as I did this exercise was my tendency to hang on to the facts of how I was hurt more than the perspectives I was learning. As unhealthy feelings and thoughts would surface in my journal that looked more like proof than perspective, I would

- be honest about the feelings I was having;
- be brave enough to stop the accompanying runaway thoughts, even if I had to say that out loud;
- check possible distortions with other trusted friends or my counselor, and with the Word of God;
- find a Scripture verse that could speak truth to some part of the memory and apply God's Word to my thinking; and
- process through it until I could find a more healed way of looking at and telling my story.

It took time to get to this place. And it's okay that it will also take time for you to heal and find these healthy perspectives.

Father, when I'm tempted to run back to old patterns, help me stay strong in You. I don't want to run away, isolate, numb away the hard realities, or silence what my heart is trying to say. There is a healed version of me waiting and wanting to emerge, and I want to step into this version of me. Help me release my grudges, Lord, and entrust my hurts and life to You. In Jesus' name, amen.

CHAPTER 8

UNCHANGEABLE FEELS UNFORGIVABLE

WE'VE BEEN DOING some hard work here, friend. We've been lifting up ways we've been wounded that are hard to look at, let alone sit with and explore.

As I consider the facts of my circumstances, I find myself wishing I could go back in time to change everything that hurt me. Don't you? We want to somehow undo what's been done. But so much of what has happened is unchangeable, and unchangeable can sometimes feel unforgivable.

The key, however, is to remember we are not powerless.

We can work to make peace with those things that can never be changed. And we can discover the possibilities for how what has happened can change *us*—for the better, not the worse.

For me, it was unchangeable fact that Art had been unfaithful. And I had to realize that it could change me in good or bad ways. It could be used for God's glory or my family's detriment.

Everything we experience has the possibility to change us. Painful experiences can especially be catalysts for transformation.

Maybe you haven't even dared to think past the hurt. But what if you could not only think past the hurt but *dream* past the hurt?

The tenderness in your heart can make you more aware of others. The experiential wisdom you've gained can be so life-giving to those you encounter who need help. The journey of healing and

forgiveness could very well be pointing you in the direction of a newfound purpose for your life. Please know, I still wish with all my heart that some of the pain my family has walked through wasn't part of our story. But it is.

So now I have to make the choice to let it be used for good.

We have important choices to make. What will we do with what we have—in our stories and in our hearts? Where do we want to go from here?

Anger is an acid that can do more harm to the vessel in which it is stored than to anything on which it is poured.

—MARK TWAIN

KEEP

Forgiveness is a hard step to take; it's also the
only step that leads to anything good. Every other
choice—including the choice to not do anything and
remain where we are—just adds more hurt upon hurt.

———

Forgiveness doesn't let the other person off the
hook. It actually places them in God's hands.

———

We don't serve a do-nothing God.
He is always working.

———

Grief finds all of us.

———

Forgiveness doesn't always fix relationships,
but it does help mend the hurting heart.

———

There is nothing more powerful than a
person living what God's Word teaches.

Write any other sentences that spoke to you from chapter 8 of
Forgiving What You Can't Forget:

....

....

....

....

....

....

....

READ

Commit everything you do to the LORD.
Trust him, and he will help you.
—PSALM 37:5 NLT

As far as it depends on you, live at peace with everyone.
Do not take revenge, my dear friends, but leave room for
God's wrath, for it is written: "It is mine to avenge; I will
repay," says the Lord. On the contrary: "If your enemy is
hungry, feed him; if he is thirsty, give him something to
drink. In doing this, you will heap burning coals on his head."
Do not be overcome by evil, but overcome evil with good.
—ROMANS 12:18–21

Be kind and compassionate to one another, forgiving
each other, just as in Christ God forgave you.
—EPHESIANS 4:32

Put on the full armor of God, so that you can take your
stand against the devil's schemes. For our struggle is not
against flesh and blood, but against the rulers, against
the authorities, against the powers of this dark world and
against the spiritual forces of evil in the heavenly realms.
—EPHESIANS 6:11–12

Casting all your cares [all your anxieties, all your
worries, and all your concerns, once and for all]
on Him, for He cares about you [with deepest
affection, and watches over you very carefully].
—1 PETER 5:7 AMP

Have you ever despised yourself based on what someone else did to harm you? Write your thoughts below.

Do you find yourself constantly bracing for impact? Why do you think that is?

What is "an unchangeable situation" in your life that makes you feel like healing is more challenging?

We find ourselves questioning what forgiveness would even accomplish in this kind of situation. It seems like forgiveness shouldn't apply here. But in reality, forgiveness is always the only step that leads to anything good. Every other choice—including doing nothing and remaining where we are—just adds more hurt upon hurt.

With this in mind, what do you think forgiveness would accomplish in your "unchangeable situation"? Can you be specific?

....
....
....
....
....
....

Is there someone you're unable to reconcile with that you need to forgive?

....
....
....
....
....
....

Here are a few truths I've been learning to hang on to in my heart when I'm struggling to step toward forgiveness. Take some time to reflect on these statements and write a few thoughts about each of them:

- Forgiveness is more satisfying than revenge.

....
....

- Our God is not a do-nothing God.

....

....

- Your offender is also suffering from pain.

....

....

- The purpose of forgiveness is not always reconciliation.

....

....

- The enemy is the real villain.

....

....

How can you use these five truths to help you make progress and move forward?

....

....

....

....

....

....

Your heartbreak is real. But you can still choose your actions and reactions. Your choice to forgive and the resulting peace in your life will keep this pain from becoming a perpetual cycle—from you and then going out to others. "As far as it depends on you, live at peace with everyone. . . . Do not be overcome by evil, but overcome evil with good" (Romans 12:18, 21). What does it look like for you to live this out right now? Who could benefit from you stopping the cycle of pain in your life?

....

....

....

....

....

Painful experiences can be catalysts for transformation. How could the unchangeable experiences of your past change you for the better and impact your future for good?

....

....

....

....

....

A Note from Lysa

Some people may associate forgiveness with weakness, like it's a sign someone is passive or lacking self-respect. But research shows that forgiveness helps people regain a sense of power after being hurt.[1] When someone wounds us, we're left in shock over something we had no control over. When we choose to forgive, we're refusing to remain in a state of powerlessness. We're reclaiming what has felt lost by taking the initiative to redirect our lives.

*Forgiveness is
the economy of
the heart . . .
forgiveness saves the
expense of anger,
the cost of hatred,
the waste of spirits.*

—HANNAH MORE

PRAY

*Father, none of this is simple. Help me sit with
these truths and let them eventually change me. I
trust You are working in me and in the people and
circumstances that have caused great pain in my
life. My past, present, and future are Yours, Lord. I
pray I will remember and walk out these truths as I
draw closer to You. In Jesus' name, amen.*

CHAPTER 9

BOUNDARIES THAT HELP US STOP DANCING WITH DYSFUNCTION

THE PEOPLE I CARE about make a personal impact on me. The happenings in their lives ripple over into my life. When they rejoice, I rejoice. When they mourn, I mourn. Our hearts are connected.

But when the consequences of their choices become like tidal waves continually knocking me over . . . it deeply affects me. While I'm trying to love them the best I can, I know something that keeps happening here is wrong. Maybe I'm just putting myself in the wrong place, too close to the waves? Whatever it is, I have to figure it out and stop the pattern.

Have you been there too?

When someone's choices keep putting us on guard, it can feel like we're never progressing past emotional survival mode. If there's ever a time to get serious about managing our emotional energy and getting rid of relational habits that hinder us, this is it. If we want to have a shot at being healthy enough to walk the road of forgiveness, we have to better manage the relationships that seem to be wearing us out.

This means identifying what bankrupts our spiritual capacity. What leaves us utterly zapped of self-control, gentleness, and compassion? Are we exhausting our personal resources by trying to help someone who continues to make hurtful or destructive choices?

Is there something that's causing us to feel continually wounded? Even with good intentions, is there any part of this where we're trying to control someone else's out-of-control behavior? How can we keep this from happening?

By creating wise boundaries for ourselves.

We're not being selfish or cruel here. We're not being manipulative or mean-spirited. Actually, setting boundaries is often one of the most loving things to do. We're setting ourselves up to be strong and healthy so we can continue loving and respecting people. If our hearts keep ending up in places where they get stomped on, we need to prevent that from happening. If we're struggling to manage our own actions and reactions, we need to own our limitations and communicate them in honoring ways.

We need to be freer to direct more energy toward healthy behaviors. Because healthy people can be forgiving people.

KEEP

I cannot control things out of my control.

———

Most of us would agree that it isn't really
possible to change another person.

———

Forgiveness releases our need for retaliation,
not our need for boundaries.

———

Compassion is key to forgiveness.

———

What we allow is what we will live.

———

It's for the sake of your sanity that you draw
necessary boundaries. It's for the sake of stability
that you stay consistent with those boundaries.

———

Maybe it's time to re-educate some people
in our lives with clearly stated, gracefully
implemented, consistently kept boundaries.

———

The purpose of boundaries isn't to keep the other
person away; it's to help keep yourself together.

Write any other sentences that spoke to you from chapter 9 of
Forgiving What You Can't Forget:

....

....

....

....

Do not let wisdom and understanding out
of your sight, preserve sound judgment and
discretion; they will be life for you.

—PROVERBS 3:21–22

"Let your 'yes' mean 'yes,' and your 'no' mean 'no.'"

—MATTHEW 5:37 CSB

Love must be sincere. Hate what is evil; cling to what
is good. Be devoted to one another in love. Honor one
another above yourselves. Never be lacking in zeal,
but keep your spiritual fervor, serving the Lord. Be
joyful in hope, patient in affliction, faithful in prayer.

—ROMANS 12:9–12

Rejoice with those who rejoice;
mourn with those who mourn.

—ROMANS 12:15

Each one should carry their own load.

—GALATIANS 6:5

Are there any misconceptions you've had about boundaries?

....
....
....
....
....

Have you ever found yourself working harder on people than they're working on themselves?

In chapter 9 of *Forgiving What You Can't Forget*, I wrote, "Even if I get them off these tracks in this moment, they'll climb right back on them tomorrow." What does this statement mean to you?

....
....
....
....
....

How do you want people to treat you?

....
....
....
....
....

What do you need to change to communicate this and really implement necessary boundaries?

....

....

....

....

....

Read Romans 12:9–12: "Love must be sincere. Hate what is evil; cling to what is good. Be devoted to one another in love. Honor one another above yourselves. Never be lacking in zeal, but keep your spiritual fervor, serving the Lord. Be joyful in hope, patient in affliction, faithful in prayer."

Write down the behaviors in these verses that you could live out more consistently if you established healthier boundaries in your life.

....

....

....

....

....

Think of one particularly challenging relationship in your life where forgiveness seems quite difficult. Maybe the other person involved is constantly frustrating you, hurting your feelings, or making unrealistic demands of you. Answer these questions as you think about some necessary boundaries you may need to put in place with this relationship.

What kind of person do you want to be, not just in this relationship but consistently in all your relationships?

....
....
....

What do you need to do in this relationship to stay consistent in your character, conduct, and communication?

....
....
....
....
....

How would you define these terms?
Emotional capacity:

....
....
....
....

Spiritual capacity:

....
....
....
....

What are some areas of your life where you have the most limitations with your capacity (at your job, in parenting, during the holidays, etc.)?

....
....
....
....
....

Based on your realistic assessment of capacity, how does this relationship threaten to hyperextend what you can realistically and even generously give?

....
....
....
....
....

Do you feel the freedom in this relationship to communicate what you can and cannot give without the fear of being punished or pushed away? Why or why not? Based on your reasons, is there an action step you need to take in this situation?

....
....
....
....
....
....

What are some realistic restrictions you can place on yourself to reduce the access this person has to your most limited emotional or physical resources?

....
....
....
....
....
....

What time of the day is the healthiest for you to interact with this person?

....

What time of the day is the unhealthiest for you to interact with this person?

....

In what ways is this person's unpredictable behavior negatively impacting your trust in God, your other relationships, your job, your home life, or your sense of hope for the future?

....
....
....
....
....
....

How are you suffering the consequences for their choices more than they are?

. . . .

. . . .

. . . .

. . . .

. . . .

What are their most realistic and most unrealistic expectations of you? What are your most realistic and most unrealistic expectations of them?

. . . .

. . . .

. . . .

. . . .

. . . .

What boundaries do you need to put in place?

. . . .

. . . .

. . . .

. . . .

. . . .

A Note from Lysa

Pain is a reminder that the real enemy is trying to take us out and bring us down by keeping us stuck in broken places.

Pain is an indication that a transformation is needed. There is a weakness where new strength needs to enter in.

How do we get this new strength? How do we stop ourselves from chasing what will numb us when the deepest parts of us scream for relief? How do we survive the piercing pain of this minute, this hour?

We invite God's closeness.

James 4:8 reminds us that when we draw near to God, He will draw near to us. When we invite Him close, He always accepts our invitation. Psalm 91:1 says, "Whoever dwells in the shelter of the Most High will rest in the shadow of the Almighty." He can become a haven for us, calming our hearts as we trust in Him.

And so we turn our eyes to Him and pray. No matter how vast our pit, prayer is big enough to fill us with the realization of His presence like nothing else.

Will you pray with me now?

Lord, draw me close to You.

Help me remember what is true. I am not alone, because You are with me. I am not weak, because Your strength is infused in me. I am not empty, because I'm drinking daily from Your fullness. You are my dwelling place. And in You I have shelter from every stormy circumstance and harsh reality. I'm not pretending the hard things don't exist, but I am rejoicing in the fact that Your covering protects me and prevents those hard things from affecting me like they used to.

You, the Most High, have the final say over me. You know me and love me intimately. And today I declare that I will trust You in the midst of my pain. You are my everyday dwelling place, my saving grace. In Jesus' name, amen.

CHAPTER 10

BECAUSE THEY THOUGHT GOD WOULD SAVE THEM

I'VE SEEN GOD do amazing things.

I'm sure you have your own stories that put His goodness and glory on display. If we were sitting together at the gray table today, I'd be honored to hear every one of them.

Seeing those things strengthens our faith. But they can also leave us wondering why He isn't doing those kinds of amazing things in our lives *now*.

Have you ever asked some hard questions about God? I have not only asked hard questions but have found myself being disillusioned by the heartbreak causing me to wrestle in these ways.

After spending so much time feeling disoriented in my circumstances, confusion turned into disillusionment, and disillusionment turned into hopelessness.

I'd prayed and seen nothing change. I seemed to be surrounded by proof that He wasn't working. That He had no plan. The more skeptical of His faithfulness I became, the more resistant to forgiveness I felt.

This is what happens when we forget that our earthly perspective is like looking through a keyhole, while God sees the entire room. Without seeing the full picture, we're drawing conclusions from the limiting view of our pain.

Our limited and broken perception is not evidence of God **not** keeping His promises. Our feelings in one season of life won't last forever and don't prove what God's character is.

Have we been thinking about it all wrong? Have we just been too caught up in our unmet expectations? Our definition of *good*? Our time line?

In the midst of all the unknowns, we *do* know He has shown Himself trustworthy. In the midst of feeling lost, we can look up to Him. He can point us to what's true when we can't sense it ourselves. He can guide us in walking in His life-giving ways and help us hang on until we can see more of the good He already sees.

KEEP

The most devastating spiritual crisis isn't when we
wonder why God isn't doing something. It's when
we become utterly convinced He no longer cares.

———

What makes faith fall apart isn't doubt. It's
becoming too certain of the wrong things.

———

Today isn't the whole story. Today is part of
the story, but it's not the whole story.

———

God's silence is not proof of His absence.

———

Forgiveness, even in the midst of all the unknowns, is
the way we stay in step with the beat of God's heart.

———

What if, from God's perspective, what we
are asking for is not at all what we'd want if
we could see everything from His complete,
eternal, perfect vantage point?

Write any other sentences that spoke to you from chapter 10 of
Forgiving What You Can't Forget:

Trust in the LORD with all your heart and lean not on your own understanding; in all your ways submit to him, and he will make your paths straight.

—PROVERBS 3:5-6

"My thoughts are not your thoughts, neither are your ways my ways," declares the LORD. "As the heavens are higher than the earth, so are my ways higher than your ways and my thoughts than your thoughts."

—ISAIAH 55:8-9

"Very truly I tell you, you will weep and mourn while the world rejoices. You will grieve, but your grief will turn to joy. A woman giving birth to a child has pain because her time has come; but when her baby is born she forgets the anguish because of her joy that a child is born into the world. So with you: Now is your time of grief, but I will see you again and you will rejoice, and no one will take away your joy."

—JOHN 16:20-22

Oh, praise the greatness of our God! He is the
Rock, his works are perfect, and all his ways
are just. A faithful God who does no wrong.

—DEUTERONOMY 32:3–4

How abundant are the good things that you
have stored up for those who fear you.

—PSALM 31:19

We're going to explore some of our hard questions about God and how we might be able to look at our story from a different angle. As we do that, let's keep a few things in mind.

The enemy wants us to believe that what we feel is the only reality and that what we see is the full picture. But God constantly reminds us in His Word to think differently about what we perceive:

- "Faith is confidence in what we hope for and assurance about what we do not see" (Hebrews 11:1).
- "Set your minds on things above, not on earthly things" (Colossians 3:2).
- "We fix our eyes not on what is seen, but on what is unseen, since what is seen is temporary, but what is unseen is eternal" (2 Corinthians 4:18).

What we see in this world will not be forever. What is in front of us right now is not the whole story.

The character of God does not change while we are hurting and confused. The mercy of God weeps, the justice of God will have the final say, and the love of God will somehow work divine good even from evil.

I've listed some hard questions about God below. Journal your thoughts about them along with any positive perspective shifts this chapter of *Forgiving What You Can't Forget* is helping you make.

I've filled in the first one to give you an example.

Why did God let this happen?

OLD THINKING:

Maybe God isn't sensitive to how much this hurts . . . or worse yet, maybe He doesn't care.

NEW PERSPECTIVE SHIFT:

God is deeply compassionate and absolutely cares about me. He doesn't cause evil. We live in a sin-filled world where bad things will happen because of that sin. But God can take even this and bring about good in the midst of all that's hard.

WHAT I'M STILL TRYING TO PRAYERFULLY PROCESS:

I must keep looking for evidences of God's faithfulness in this process. And I must realize that my expectations of how this should all turn out may not line up with God's plans. That's where it's crucial that I trust Him with all that is happening today and realize my job is to be obedient to God. God's job is everything else.

How in the world could this ever be used for good when nothing about it seems good now?

OLD THINKING:

NEW PERSPECTIVE SHIFT:

WHAT I'M STILL TRYING TO PRAYERFULLY PROCESS:

....

....

....

....

And if He is all powerful, why didn't He stop this from happening?

OLD THINKING:

....

....

....

....

NEW PERSPECTIVE SHIFT:

....

....

....

....

WHAT I'M STILL TRYING TO PRAYERFULLY PROCESS:

....

....

....

....

He could do a miracle today and change
everything . . . so why isn't He?

OLD THINKING:

....
....
....
....

NEW PERSPECTIVE SHIFT:

....
....
....
....

WHAT I'M STILL TRYING TO PRAYERFULLY PROCESS:

....
....
....
....

Where can you look back and see God's faithfulness in a past
situation that caused you to question Him at the time?

....
....
....
....

My counselor says, "Hope is the melody of the future. Faith is dancing to that melody right now." What would it look like for you to live this out?

....
....
....
....

In John 16:20, Jesus said, "Your grief will turn to joy." How are you seeing glimpses of this? If you're having trouble seeing instances of grief turning to joy, write a prayer out to the Lord, asking Him to start revealing how this is true in your circumstances.

....
....
....
....
....
....

In what ways are you only looking at your life from your own perspective? How might it change things if you trusted that God's perspective is different?

....
....
....
....
....
....

"What if I've been thinking of this all wrong?" When you read this chapter of *Forgiving What You Can't Forget*, how did this question cause you to reconsider some things about a specific person or situation?

....

....

....

....

A Note from Lysa

One of my dear friends, Jennie Lusko, lost her precious five-year-old daughter to an asthma attack a few days before Christmas in 2012. It took me years of knowing her before I could ask her a question that had been rattling around inside of me.

"After Lenya passed, how did you drive away from that hospital?" I'd heard she did. I'd known she somehow found the strength to do what I think most of us would have such a hard time doing. Though the emotional shock and devastation were completely overwhelming, she started moving forward by driving home that first night. She said goodbye. I don't fully know step by step how. But I know why because of her answer to my question:

"My worst day was my daughter's best day."

And in her words I heard the collision of heaven and earth. I know Jennie wishes with everything in her that this had never happened. Of course she does. Just like I wish the affair had never happened. The losses here on earth feel so very final.

Until we remember there's more to the story that only God knows. There's a heavenly reality mixed with every earthly finality that is the truest makings of hope.

What if it's hard for me to hear the collision of heaven and earth in my own story because the hurt screams too loud?

What if my trying to discern the fairness of God is missing the point?

Instead of making assumptions that dismantle my faith, I could recall the goodness of His character and build my faith.

There's more to the story that only God knows. As I sit with this, I realize that my view is limited. No matter what I may conclude from my view, and no matter what my pain is telling me, I can hope in what is eternally true: He is good, and He is always working to make good things happen.

*If you'd like to read more about Jennie's story, check out her book *The Fight to Flourish* (Thomas Nelson, 2020).

PRAY

Father, I admit I have made wrong assumptions about my circumstances and about You as well. I have also held on to false perspectives stemming from my limited view. What if I've been thinking of this all wrong? Help me see things the way You see them. Help me trust You are good and that You are good to me. In Jesus' name, amen.

All I have seen teaches me to trust the Creator for all I have not seen.

—RALPH WALDO EMERSON

We win by
tenderness.
We conquer
by forgiveness.

—FREDERICK WILLIAM
ROBERTSON

CHAPTER 11

FORGIVING GOD

IF YOU AND I WERE at a coffee shop, we'd each place an order. Mine would be an extra-hot latte with almond milk and one stevia. You'd have your own specific request. Shortly afterward, we'd get exactly what we asked for (or we'd keep asking until we did).

I don't know about you, but this can become my approach to prayer. I expect an infinite God to reduce His vast ways of doing things down to only what I can think up and pray for. And when I don't see the results I'm expecting, I'm sometimes crushed and confused.

I don't even consider if I'm interpreting what I'm seeing correctly.

Do you do this too?

We're just feeling the ache of a need and naturally filling in the blank of what we think the answer to our prayers should be. When things don't turn out the way we hoped, we can find ourselves questioning God's love and faithfulness.

When our trust in God gets shaken, it's hard to walk the road of forgiveness.

In our bewilderment we are forgetting that if the good we expected isn't here yet, we must trust there's something God knows that we don't, as we learned in the last chapter. He sees the bigger picture we can't.

It's so hard for me to remember this. That's why I've started opening my hands when I pray. Lifting up open hands is my physical reminder that I truly trust God.

God's faithfulness isn't demonstrated by His activity aligning with our prayers. It's when our prayers align with His faithfulness that we become more assured of His activity.

So let's try to process this and change our very human-oriented approach to prayer together. We should absolutely come to God with our needs, desires, and cries of our heart. But we should also let His faithfulness build our trust and ease the ache of our confusion. And then try to look at what's right in front of us in light of what we know to be true of Him.

KEEP

We see only what the human mind can imagine.
God is building something we cannot even fathom.

———

When I was saying God wasn't answering my
prayers, what I was really saying was God
wasn't doing what I wanted Him to do.

———

God does some of His best work in the unseen.

———

What things look like from an earthly
perspective, God sees differently.

Write any other sentences that spoke to you from chapter 11 of *Forgiving What You Can't Forget*:

He humbled you, causing you to hunger and
then feeding you with manna, which neither you
nor your ancestors had known, to teach you that
man does not live on bread alone but on every
word that comes from the mouth of the LORD.

—DEUTERONOMY 8:3

"I am the bread of life. Whoever comes
to me will never go hungry, and whoever
believes in me will never be thirsty."

—JOHN 6:35

"I am the living bread that came down from heaven.
Whoever eats this bread will live forever. This bread is
my flesh, which I will give for the life of the world."

—JOHN 6:51

"The Advocate, the Holy Spirit, whom the Father
will send in my name, will teach you all things and
will remind you of everything I have said to you."

—JOHN 14:26

Who then is the one who condemns? No
one. Christ Jesus who died—more than that,
who was raised to life—is at the right hand
of God and is also interceding for us.

—ROMANS 8:34

Though we live in the world, we do not wage war as
the world does. The weapons we fight with are not
the weapons of the world. On the contrary, they have
divine power to demolish strongholds. We demolish
arguments and every pretension that sets itself up
against the knowledge of God, and we take captive
every thought to make it obedient to Christ.

—2 CORINTHIANS 10:3–5

"Give us this day our daily bread" is more than just a request for what we think we need in order to survive whatever we're facing today. It's acknowledging that God's will is best so that we will see His good provision in what He gives us—whether that good is for today or part of a much bigger plan.

This includes the days when what we see in front of us is extremely confusing and difficult. It's all still part of what God will use for eventual good, if we will only trust Him.

Praying this way shifts our focus from asking only for what we want to trusting God to provide what we actually need.

Jesus said, "If you, then . . . know how to give good gifts to your children, how much more will your Father in heaven give good gifts to those who ask him!" (Matthew 7:11).

God is our generous provider and loving Father. And He knows what is good better than anyone. This is truth, regardless of what our perspective allows us to see.

Thinking through all of this has helped me realize I might be looking at answered prayers—God's provision—all wrong.

I know this isn't easy to wrestle through. But we want to learn how to trust Him more and walk into the good things He has for us. Keep that in mind as you work through the next several questions.

Have you ever expected God to do things exactly as you were praying for them to be done? Journal your thoughts about finding a better balance between praying for the exact outcome you've been wanting and praying for God's will to be done even if it's different from what you want.

It's not at all wrong to ask God for what we want. Just as a child asks their parents for what they want, we can ask our loving Father. But then we must trust God's answer, even if the outcome doesn't line up with our desire. Where might you need to change up some things you've been praying for?

We are living answered prayers today. Where do you see this being true in your life?

When we say God isn't answering our prayers, we are really saying God isn't doing what we want Him to do. How does this encourage you or frustrate you?

....
....
....
....

How does this help you make peace with something you've been struggling through?

....
....
....
....

How do these perspective changes help you make peace with what God allows?

....
....
....
....

What is something you've been crying over, asking God to change, that might actually be His protection or unexpected provision?

....
....
....
....

Never does the human soul appear so strong as when it foregoes revenge and dares to forgive an injury.

—EDWIN HUBBEL CHAPIN

Father, every day You are protecting me and providing for me. Every day You are there. And whether I recognize it or not, I am living in answered prayers. Today I will look at what's right in front of me through what I know to be true about You, God. Today is a gift, even if some circumstances feel the exact opposite. God, I know You aren't causing these hard things, but You will take them and eventually use them for good. While this is still hard for me to wrestle through at times, I will keep holding on to my faith in You. And I can trust You to make my story one of beautiful redemption. In Jesus' name, amen.

CHAPTER 12

THE PART THAT LOSS PLAYS

LOSS IS INESCAPABLE in this life. We've all felt its sting in big ways and small. And it's only natural that as we process each of our losses that grief is a major part of what must be worked through.

I'm learning not only how to grieve my losses but also how to recognize a blessing of grief: it can make our hearts tender. Soft hearts breed compassion. Compassionate hearts breed forgiveness. And it's not only my grief that leads to all this good cultivation of the heart. Leaning into other people's grief can do the same thing.

When we encounter someone else's loss, the sacred nature of grief ripples into our lives. We find ourselves grieving along with them because we're no strangers to human hurt.

Sitting in the fresh grief of loss (ours or someone else's) makes us all realize how very human we are—how very fragile life is and how we really shouldn't hold on to the stuff that makes us resentful. It's not worth it to taint the beauty of life with bitterness.

Most of us carry bitterness not because we want to but because we've had something or someone take from us unfairly. What started with love and trust turned into loss and sorrow. Our emptiness left room for the bitterness to sneak in. And as bitterness lingers, it hardens our hearts.

It's difficult to forgive and heal when the rock-solid hardness of bitterness won't budge.

But just like hardened, parched soil can be softened and tilled, our hearts can become tender again too. As the tears from grief fall, the soil of our hearts softens. That softening is the unexpected gift of grief. Loss always seems like an end until we see beautiful beginnings start to sprout from a softened, tender heart.

KEEP

If loss was the way bitterness got in, maybe
revisiting grief will help provide a way out.

———

Bitterness doesn't just want to room with you; it
wants to completely consume everything about you.

———

Bitterness wears the disguises of other
chaotic emotions that are harder to
attribute to the original source of hurt.

———

Hardened hearts have such a propensity to get
shattered. Soft hearts don't as easily break.

———

Undealt-with hurt and pain hardens like parched soil.
And the only way to soften it afresh is for the tears
to fall soft and liquid and free-flowing once again.

Write any other sentences that spoke to you from chapter 12 of
Forgiving What You Can't Forget:

....

....

....

....

....

....

....

....

Joseph went up to bury his father. . . . When they reached the threshing floor of Atad, near the Jordan, they lamented loudly and bitterly; and there Joseph observed a seven-day period of mourning for his father.

—GENESIS 50:7, 10

When Job's three friends . . . heard about all the troubles that had come upon him, they set out from their homes and met together by agreement to go and sympathize with him and comfort him. When they saw him from a distance, they could hardly recognize him; they began to weep aloud, and they tore their robes and sprinkled dust on their heads. Then they sat on the ground with him for seven days and seven nights. No one said a word to him, because they saw how great his suffering was.

—JOB 2:11–13

Weep with those who weep.

—ROMANS 12:15 ESV

The heart of the wise is in the house of mourning, but the heart of fools is in the house of pleasure.

—ECCLESIASTES 7:4

How do the following revelations about bitterness encourage you?

1. Bitterness doesn't have a core of hate but rather a core of hurt.
2. Bitterness isn't usually found most deeply in those whose hearts are hard but rather those who are most tender.
3. Bitterness isn't an indication of limited potential in relationships.

We're going to look through some signs of bitterness that can help us start to recognize bitterness in ourselves. Make no mistake, I am right here with you trying to identify bitterness in myself.

We can't address it if we don't acknowledge it.

Remember that condemnation is not from the Lord, but feeling conviction to let God address something with us is good. So if you're feeling defeated already, pray something like this: *God, I know You want to rescue me from anything distracting me from living Your truth. Draw my heart close and show me what to do from here.*

> Place a check mark beside each of the following
> indicators of hidden bitterness you see in yourself.

- ☐ Derogatory assumptions
- ☐ Sharp, cutting comments
- ☐ A grudge that feels increasingly heavy inside you
- ☐ The desire for the one who hurt you to suffer
- ☐ Anxiety around the unfairness of other people's happiness
- ☐ Skepticism that most people can't be trusted
- ☐ Cynicism about the world in general
- ☐ Negativity cloaked as you having a more realistic view than others
- ☐ Resentment toward others whom you perceive moved on too quickly
- ☐ Frustrations with God for not doling out severe enough consequences
- ☐ Seething anger over the unfairness of it all that grows more intense over time
- ☐ Obsessing over what happened by replaying the surrounding events over and over
- ☐ Making passive-aggressive statements to prove a point
- ☐ One-upping other people's sorrow or heartbreak to show your pain is worse
- ☐ Feeling justified in behaviors you know aren't healthy because of how wronged you've been
- ☐ Snapping and exploding on other people whose offenses don't warrant that kind of reaction
- ☐ Becoming unexplainably withdrawn in situations you used to enjoy
- ☐ Disconnecting from innocent people because of the fear of being hurt again
- ☐ Irrational assumptions of worst-case scenarios

- ☐ Having unrealistic expectations
- ☐ Refusing to tell the person who hurt you what's really bothering you
- ☐ Stiff-arming people who don't think the same way you do
- ☐ Rejecting opportunities to come together and talk about things
- ☐ Refusing to consider other perspectives
- ☐ Blaming and shaming the other person inside your mind over and over
- ☐ Covertly recruiting others to your side under the guise of processing or venting

Again, there isn't an ounce of desire in my heart to evoke any kind of condemnation or throw any sort of guilt in your direction. Not at all. I'm too busy managing my own emotions around this list. But I do want to become more aware of what's affecting me. And I believe this could help you too.

Journal how the indicators you've checked are becoming part of how you're thinking or speaking right now.

....

....

....

....

Are there any other disguised issues you can think of that could have bitterness at the root?

....

....

....

....

In this chapter of *Forgiving What You Can't Forget*, we read, "Bitterness doesn't have a core of hate but rather hurt." Journal your thoughts about this statement.

....

....

....

....

Ecclesiastes 7:2 tells us, "It is better to go to a house of mourning than to go to a house of feasting, for death is the destiny of everyone; the living should take this to heart."

Grief from someone's death always has profound lessons for those still living. I've never heard of someone regretting forgiveness as they leave this earth, but I have heard the sobs of unforgiveness.

I want to take these lessons to heart, because it can make a good difference in how I live, especially as I think about forgiveness. What kind of life lessons related to this come to mind for you?

....

....

....

....

Our forgiving love toward men is the evidence of God's forgiving love in us.

—ANDREW MURRAY

In this chapter of *Forgiving What You Can't Forget*, we read, "Bitterness is in part unprocessed grief, so it only makes sense that, by sitting in a part of the grief process of another, we can revisit the processing of our own losses." Reflect on a time when you have allowed the grief of another to speak to you and soften your heart. Describe how it affected you.

In what ways would you like for your heart to soften right now?

Who in your life is experiencing some kind of grief? How might you be able to open yourself to it?

How did the Jewish traditions taught in this chapter of *Forgiving What You Can't Forget* inspire or challenge you? What would you like to implement in your life as a result?

....

....

....

....

Another quote from this same chapter is, "What if bitterness is actually a seed of beautiful potential not yet planted in the rich soil of forgiveness?" Journal your thoughts here.

....

....

....

....

PRAY

Father, I don't want any bitterness to consume me. I want to let tenderness into the hardened places of my heart. Help me grow soft, help me grieve what needs to be grieved, and let others' reactions to loss teach me something without growing bitter myself. I desperately want to live with the sweetness of possibility in my everyday life without the pain of my past getting in the way. Thank You for showing me how to do this. In Jesus' name, amen.

CHAPTER 13

BITTERNESS IS A BAD DEAL THAT MAKES BIG PROMISES

ONCE I STARTED noticing bitterness in myself, I couldn't believe how much it was negatively impacting me.

Sometimes it'd be an overall sense of heaviness and unsettledness, eating away at my peace.

Other times, even the slightest offenses would send me into a tailspin of emotion that I neither expected nor wanted. No one wants their day hijacked by a flood of hurt feelings.

Regardless, I didn't realize it was hidden bitterness that was skewing my perspective and tainting my interpretations, keeping me chained to the undealt-with woundings of my past.

This pervasive bitterness was evidence of unforgiveness. Me not forgiving people who hurt me was me agreeing to bring the pain they caused into every present-day situation I was in—hurting me over and over again. And not just me, but everyone around me.

Maybe you've seen some of this in your life too.

You and I don't really want the chaos bitterness brings. What we really want is the healing forgiveness allows.

If we follow the bitterness down to the root, we'll find what we need to forgive.

We'll see what we need to entrust to God and how to take the next step forward.

And once we do that, we can receive something even better

than feeling vindicated. Peace. Wholeness. The ability to bring the atmosphere of peace wherever we go.

Peace with God, with ourselves, with others.

Is this an unrealistic wish? No. It's the will of God. A picture of His beauty.

Is this impossible? Yes, absolutely, if we're on our own. But it's exactly what God wants to empower us to do. We can because He can.

So let's turn the page and continue to make progress together.

Our reactions are manipulated by the lens of
unresolved past hurts. Bitter lens. Bitter reaction.

———

Bitterness isn't just a label we place on
people and the feelings around the hurts they
cause. It is like liquid acid seeping into every
part of us and corrupting all it touches.

———

Humanity without humility makes
true forgiveness impossible.

———

When the impossible is made possible
because of Jesus in us, there's no greater
testimony that can be shared.

———

Peace in my life isn't being prevented by other
people's choices. It's made possible by my choices.

———

Peace is the evidence of a life of forgiveness.

Write any other sentences that spoke to you from chapter 13 of
Forgiving What You Can't Forget:

"Salt is good, but if it loses its saltiness, how can you make it salty again? Have salt among yourselves, and be at peace with each other."

—MARK 9:50

"The older brother became angry and refused to go in. So his father went out and pleaded with him. But he answered his father, 'Look! All these years I've been slaving for you and never disobeyed your orders. Yet you never gave me even a young goat so I could celebrate with my friends. But when this son of yours who has squandered your property with prostitutes comes home, you kill the fattened calf for him!' "'My son,' the father said, 'you are always with me, and everything I have is yours. But we had to celebrate and be glad, because this brother of yours was dead and is alive again; he was lost and is found.'"

—LUKE 15:28–32

"Peace I leave with you; my peace I give you. I do not give to you as the world gives. Do not let your hearts be troubled and do not be afraid."

—JOHN 14:27

Make every effort to live in peace with everyone and to be holy; without holiness no one will see the Lord. See to it that no one falls short of the grace of God and that no bitter root grows up to cause trouble and defile many.

—HEBREWS 12:14–15

A Note from Lysa

The enemy wants to draw us more and more into the darkness where he works and ruins people. He will make resentment attractive. He will make bitterness seem justified. And he will make all our proof seem like the most productive thoughts we can have.

But it's all a lie.

He loves it when we get so twisted up in our hurt that we do his work for him. He wants us poisoned by bitterness so he can recruit us for his revenge and lure us into making accusations.

We must resist him. We must root out our bitterness.

That means we have to stop clinging to every fact that is feeding our resentment. We must drop the weight of every strong rationale that legitimizes it.

This isn't validating the wrongs at all. It's also not agreeing that the person who hurt us shouldn't have appropriate consequences for their actions. They should be held accountable. But it is saying, "I refuse to stay helpless and angry. I refuse to let this keep festering in me, because it's controlling me and corroding my heart."

Remember, turning away from bitterness is us turning toward God. And only God has what we really want.

So it's into His hand we must release our proof that we could use as a weapon against the person who hurt us. Please hear my heart in this. It's not that we can't use examples of how we were hurt in productive conversations with this person to help them understand our perspective. But there's a big difference between using examples for the sake of healthy conversations and weaponizing our pain to cause them pain. Once the conversations have been had, it's time to consider not bringing this back up in future discussions.

What this release process looks like for you will be your own journey to take. For me, it has meant deleting messages, pictures, and, hardest of all, the mental files of examples where I can weaponize the past for whatever case I'm building today. I can retell what happened with precision in ways that condemn and reduce my offender to the confines of wrong and guilty.

And please hear me: They may absolutely be wrong and guilty. They may have been declared just that by a court of law. Or in the court of public opinion. Or maybe by no one else but our own hearts.

But what we do from here with the proof matters. We can't truly forgive while simultaneously holding on to proof we can use later.

We make our choices, and our choices make us. So let's make choices that are healthy for our journey and set us up to be able to move on. Even if it's not possible to have a productive conversation with the person who hurt us, we still need to follow these healthy patterns of releasing proof. In counseling, one of the exercises that helped me so much with people I couldn't have a discussion with—because they either were no longer in my life or weren't willing to have a conversation—was to speak to an empty chair and let my counselor guide me through this.

Let's trade our proof for perspective. Release the resentment to make room for growth. Allow what happened to mature us into people more dependent on God so we can walk out forgiveness and live in His freedom and beauty.

Are there any resentments you've been collecting that may have turned into bitter feelings? If yes, what is your bitterness related to?

....
....
....
....
....
....

In this chapter of *Forgiving What You Can't Forget*, we read, "Bitterness is a bad deal that makes big promises on the front end but delivers nothing you really want on the back end." Journal below how bitterness is a bad deal that is giving you nothing you really want in your specific situation.

....
....
....
....
....
....

How have you seen bitterness intensify your reactions?

....
....
....
....

Eugene Peterson paraphrases Matthew 5:41–44 like this: "If someone takes unfair advantage of you, use the occasion to practice the servant life. . . . Love your enemies. Let them bring out the best in you, not the worst" (THE MESSAGE). This is connected to the aim of surrendering our offenses daily, keeping our hearts swept clean of bitterness, and remaining humble even when we are hurt.

This is so hard, I know. I'm the first one to cry out that this is beyond my reach. But if we refuse to surrender our offenses to the Lord, we'll never be free from the constricting force of unforgiveness and the constraining feelings of unfairness.

We can't move in this direction until we invite God to empower us. So journal a prayer asking God to help you.

Remember that our emotions will sometimes be the very last to sign on to obedience, and that's okay.

You've already taken the first step by being honest about the bitterness you see in yourself, and you've asked God to empower you to surrender the offenses done to you. This is a beautiful step of humility.

In this chapter I shared a prayer with you that I absolutely *did not* want to pray. But I knew I needed to, and I've decided to keep praying it until the beauty and rightness of it starts to settle into me.

Join me in praying this, and then continue the prayer in the lines below, adding to it and including the specifics of your own situation.

God, I give this situation to You. I release

- *my evidence of all the reasons they were so wrong*
- *my need to see this person punished*
- *my need for an apology*
- *my need for this to feel fair*
- *my need for You to declare me right and them wrong*

Show me what I need to learn from all of this. And then give me Your peace in place of my pain.

....
....
....
....

Also in this chapter, we read, "Peace in my life isn't being prevented by other people's choices. It's made possible by my choices." Is this a new perspective you need to adopt in your life? What difference will this make for you?

....
....
....
....

PRAY

Father, I'm learning so much about myself and about You as I learn to be free from resentment and bitterness. I want to choose forgiveness, which will be evidenced by a life of peace. I no longer want my peace to be held hostage by the actions or words of others.

I don't want to wait for others to bring me peace. I want to bring an atmosphere of peace into every situation I'm placed in. I need Your help to do this, Lord. In Jesus' name, amen.

CHAPTER 14

LIVING THE PRACTICE OF FORGIVENESS EVERY DAY

I SO WISH WE were sitting side by side so we could acknowledge just how far we've come. I'm thankful I've been with you here in this journal to do the hard work of processing hurt and embracing the way of forgiveness. I truly believe the progress we've made in these pages will overflow into every part of our lives.

But since we can't be together in person, let me reach through these pixelated letters and establish a marked moment of the journey we've taken and that we'll continue to walk in. This is what I'm reading out loud over us both:

> This is forgiveness: making the decision that the ones who hurt you no longer get to limit you, label you, or project the lies they believe about themselves onto you.
>
> Somewhere along the way, they got hurt. Really, really hurt. They aren't necessarily bad people, but chances are they are unhealed people. When people have a deep wound they feel they must protect, the pain from that festering place is often what they'll project.
>
> So you must make the decision that their offense will not define you or confine you by the smallness of bitterness.

The sum total of your one incredible life must not be reduced to the limitations of living hurt. The completely delightful, beautiful, fun, and brilliant way God made you must not be tainted by someone who lost their way. The lies they wrongly believed and tried to put on you must not become a burden you carry or a script you repeat.

You've got much too much going for you to be stunted by anger, haunted by resentment, or held back by fear. Grow into God's grace by accepting it freely and giving it kindly.

Throw your arms up in victory and declare, "I'm free to forgive so that I can live!"

Do it once, twice, seventy times seven. Make it an undeniable fact you're a girl bound for heaven.

The forgiveness message you dare to declare is the evidence of Jesus in you that no soul could deny. Sing it like an anthem that the one who was crushed cannot have their joy hushed. Scatter it like confetti, coloring the blandness of surviving with the radiance of thriving. Release it like the fantastic fragrance everyone loves and always wants more of.

Now put your fingers on your pulse. Do you feel that? It's your heart beating, pumping, willing you to press onward and upward. Your future is full of possibility and new joys you don't want to miss.

So get a bit carried away dancing to that song . . . you know, the one that, when its rhythm gets turned up all the way, makes it impossible for you to stay down. And if it's not a praise song, sing to Jesus anyway.

Dance! And sing! It's time to get moving and get on with living. This, my friend, is the beauty of forgiving.

KEEP

We get used to our own dysfunctions
until we are no longer aware of just how
dysfunctional things have become.

———

Your voice matters in the matters that you're facing.

———

Maturity isn't the absence of hard stuff. Maturity
is the evidence that a person allowed the hard
stuff to work for them rather than against them.

———

The best time to forgive is before we are ever
offended. The next best time to forgive is right now.

———

The daily practice of forgiveness,
specifically as we pray the Lord's Prayer,
trains us to be mindful of God.

———

Confession breaks the cycle of chaos inside of me.
Forgiveness breaks the cycle of chaos between us.

Write any other sentences that spoke to you from chapter 14 of
Forgiving What You Can't Forget:

....

....

....

....

....

....

"This, then, is how you should pray: 'Our Father in heaven, hallowed be your name, your kingdom come, your will be done, on earth as it is in heaven. Give us today our daily bread. And forgive us our debts, as we also have forgiven our debtors. And lead us not into temptation, but deliver us from the evil one.' For if you forgive other people when they sin against you, your heavenly Father will also forgive you. But if you do not forgive others their sins, your Father will not forgive your sins."

—MATTHEW 6:9–15

Love is patient, love is kind. It does not envy, it does not boast, it is not proud. It does not dishonor others, it is not self-seeking, it is not easily angered, it keeps no record of wrongs. Love does not delight in evil but rejoices with the truth. It always protects, always trusts, always hopes, always perseveres. Love never fails.

—1 CORINTHIANS 13:4–8

Consider it pure joy, my brothers and sisters, whenever
you face trials of many kinds, because you know that
the testing of your faith produces perseverance.
Let perseverance finish its work so that you may
be mature and complete, not lacking anything.

—JAMES 1:2–4

We count as blessed those who have persevered.
You have heard of Job's perseverance and
have seen what the Lord finally brought about.
The Lord is full of compassion and mercy.

—JAMES 5:11

This is a gracious thing, when, mindful of God,
one endures sorrows while suffering unjustly.

—1 PETER 2:19 ESV

A Note from Lysa

We're learning that a key part in practicing forgiveness is keeping our hearts swept clean—staying humble enough to admit and confess where we need God's forgiveness, and then daily forgiving whatever may have made us feel wronged. Keeping our hearts swept clean protects us from the enemy and from slipping into the bitterness that can take over our thoughts and actions.

After I began thinking about this more, I started to see God's call to this task repeatedly in Scripture:

- "Do not let the sun go down while you are still angry, and do not give the devil a foothold. . . . Get rid of all bitterness, rage and anger, brawling and slander, along with every form of malice. Be kind and compassionate to one another, forgiving each other, just as in Christ God forgave you" (Ephesians 4:26–27, 31–32).
- "Submit yourselves, then, to God. Resist the devil, and he will flee from you. . . . Purify your hearts" (James 4:7–8).
- "Humble yourselves, therefore, under God's mighty hand, that he may lift you up in due time. Cast all your anxiety on him because he cares for you. Be alert and of sober mind. Your enemy the devil prowls around like a roaring lion looking for someone to devour. Resist him, standing firm in the faith" (1 Peter 5:6–9).

I became aware that I must get intentional when I go to bed every night. Isn't God gracious that He allows this teaching to be tied to something we see every night? As the sun is going down, I remember it's time for God to clean me out. I do not want to go to bed with anger or other difficult emotions sitting heavy in my heart.

What exactly are we supposed to do instead?

Psalm 4:4–5 (ESV) says, "Be angry, and do not sin; ponder in your own hearts on your beds, and be silent. . . . put your trust in the LORD."

When I lay on my bed and search my heart, I find all kinds of unsettled hurt. If I fixate on it, it could lead me to sin. Instead, if I turn my thoughts to God, He will work in my heart every time.

Psalm 36 lays out the specifics here. It warns us against overlooking our own sin, embracing what is wrong, plotting evil, and failing to act wisely or do good (vv. 2–4). This is where harbored resentment and unresolved anger takes us.

The psalmist guides us to think instead about God's love, faithfulness, righteousness, justice, abundance, delight, life, and light (vv. 5–9). When we think on these things, God will take our mess of emotions and turn it into peace. He'll shift our thoughts from our perspective to His.

I've been trying this each night. It's making me more patient during the next day because I do not want the reactions of the day to become my regrets of the night. I'm having less anxiety and feelings of angst because I'm no longer stirring up my hurt and letting it consume me.

Make a peaceful nightly ritual of being silent before God. Let Him search out your heart and ask Him to turn your thoughts to Him. Ask for His forgiveness and His presence. Ask Him to help you forgive others. Learn to savor the silence and welcome His renewal and rest.

I'm still not able to do it perfectly, but I'm getting better, and it's making a difference.

What difference would it make if you were truly praying daily in confession for forgiveness?

....
....
....
....
....
....
....
....
....

The best time to forgive is before we are ever offended. What mindset must you have to make this a reality in your life?

....
....
....
....
....
....
....
....
....

Revisit the list of behaviors that are marks of maturity and the depiction of mature people living out love in 1 Corinthians 13.

Pick one or two behaviors that you see as areas you could grow in, then list a few specific goals for yourself to help you do that.

....

....

....

....

....

....

One of the best ways I've ever discovered to align my heart with the spiritual maturity God wants me to have is to saturate my thinking and processing with the truths from His Word. That's why I developed the chart below to help me not only ingest God's Word but to digest it, making it part of how I think and how I live.

Using the designed Bible study diagrams provided, apply this method of study to each of the following scriptures. I've done the first one for you as an example.

As you do this, please realize this is just for you to process and internalize these verses for yourself. So don't fret if you are unsure of an answer; just keep going and ask God to reveal what He wants you to see. The focus here is on God's Word—not getting every blank filled in perfectly.

Instructions:

- You'll see there's a square in the center of each diagram where you can write the verse.
- On the top of the square write the theme of this verse.
- On the bottom of the square write the opposite of the theme.
- On the left side of the square, in the top section of the allotted space, write out what God wants us to do in response to this verse.

- On the bottom section of that divided left side, write out what the enemy wants us to do in response to this verse.
- On the right side of the square, write out these words with space to journal a few lines under each word:
  - *Progress*: Where am I making progress with this verse?
  - *Suppress*: Is there a situation where I am wanting to ignore this verse?
  - *Digress*: Is there a situation where I'm taking steps backward with living this verse?
  - *Regress*: Where am I living in rebellion against this verse?
  - *Confess*: Am I now aware of some confessions I need to make? (I write these out, asking God to give me a spirit of humility as I do this.)
  - *Forgiveness*: Where is someone not living this verse with me? (This is an opportunity for forgiveness.)

My example to get you started:

THEME

speak words that are beneficial not hurtful

God wants me to speak life over others

GOD WANTS

ENEMY WANTS

The enemy wants me to tear down others with my words.

VERSE Ephesians 4:29

"Do not let any unwholesome talk come out of your mouths, but only what is helpful for building others up according to their needs that [OPPOSITE] it may benefit those who listen."

words that belittle or that tarnish another person so I can feel better about me.

PROGRESS

SUPPRESS

DIGRESS

REGRESS

CONFESS

FORGIVENESS

And here are some verses to start with:

"Blessed are the pure in heart, for they will see God."
—MATTHEW 5:8

"All those who exalt themselves will be humbled,
and those who humble themselves will be exalted."
—LUKE 14:11

Do not conform to the pattern of this world, but
be transformed by the renewing of your mind.
Then you will be able to test and approve what
God's will is—his good, pleasing and perfect will.
—ROMANS 12:2

If someone is caught in a sin, you who live by
the Spirit should restore that person gently. But
watch yourselves, or you also may be tempted.
—GALATIANS 6:1

As a prisoner for the Lord, then, I urge you
to live a life worthy of the calling you have
received. Be completely humble and gentle; be
patient, bearing with one another in love.
—EPHESIANS 4:1-2

Do not let any unwholesome talk come out
of your mouths, but only what is helpful for
building others up according to their needs,
that it may benefit those who listen.
—EPHESIANS 4:29

Set your minds on things above, not on earthly things.
—COLOSSIANS 3:2

Everyone should be quick to listen, slow to speak and
slow to become angry, because human anger does
not produce the righteousness that God desires.
—JAMES 1:19-20

Humble yourselves before the Lord, and he will
lift you up. Brothers and sisters, do not slander
one another. Anyone who speaks against a brother
or sister or judges them speaks against the law
and judges it. When you judge the law, you are
not keeping it, but sitting in judgment on it.
—JAMES 4:10-11

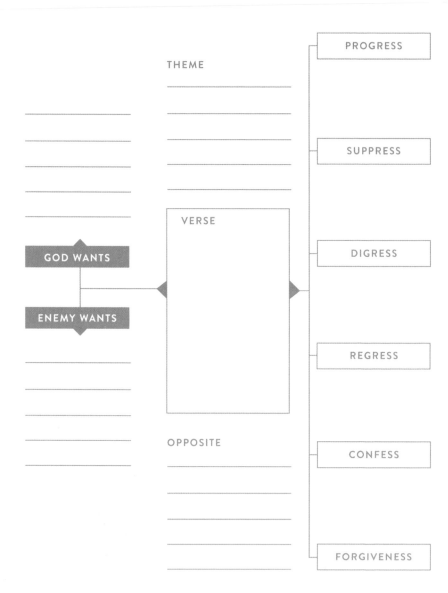

THEME

PROGRESS

SUPPRESS

VERSE

GOD WANTS

ENEMY WANTS

DIGRESS

REGRESS

OPPOSITE

CONFESS

FORGIVENESS

Find more printable worksheets of this Bible study exercise at proverbs31.org/forgiveness.

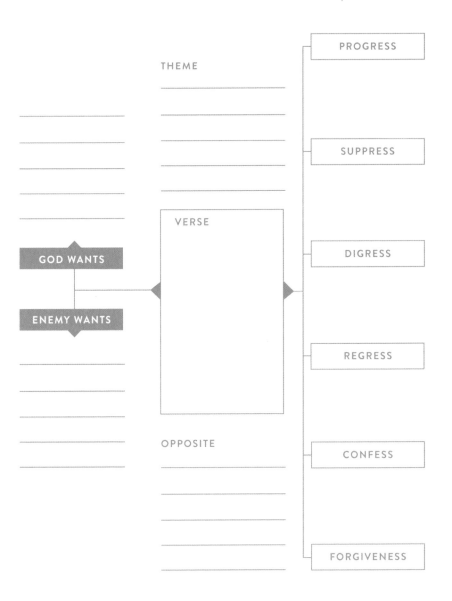

THEME

PROGRESS

SUPPRESS

VERSE

GOD WANTS

ENEMY WANTS

DIGRESS

REGRESS

OPPOSITE

CONFESS

FORGIVENESS

Find more printable worksheets of this Bible study exercise at proverbs31.org/forgiveness.

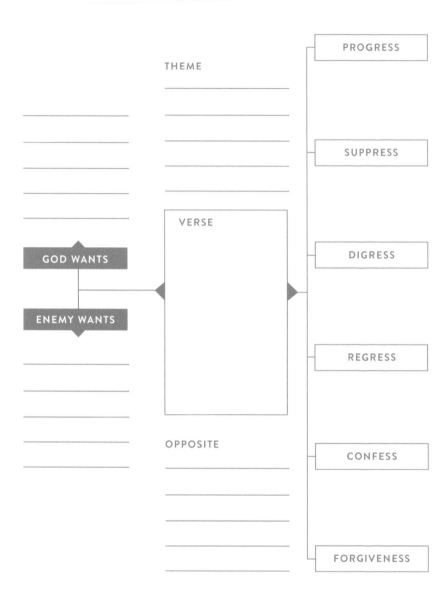

THEME

PROGRESS

SUPPRESS

VERSE

GOD WANTS

DIGRESS

ENEMY WANTS

REGRESS

OPPOSITE

CONFESS

FORGIVENESS

Find more printable worksheets of this Bible study exercise at proverbs31.org/forgiveness.

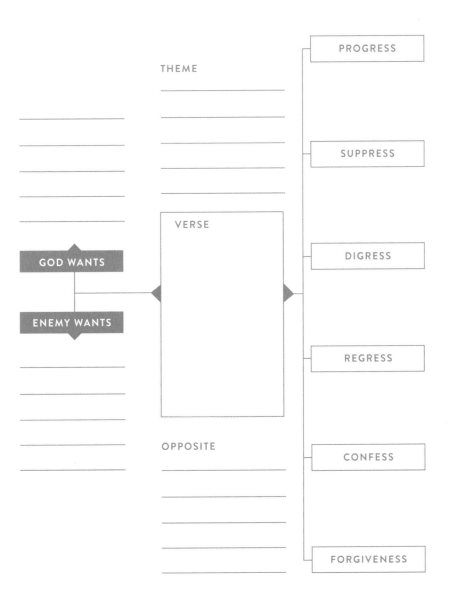

THEME

VERSE

GOD WANTS

ENEMY WANTS

OPPOSITE

PROGRESS

SUPPRESS

DIGRESS

REGRESS

CONFESS

FORGIVENESS

Find more printable worksheets of this Bible study exercise at proverbs31.org/forgiveness.

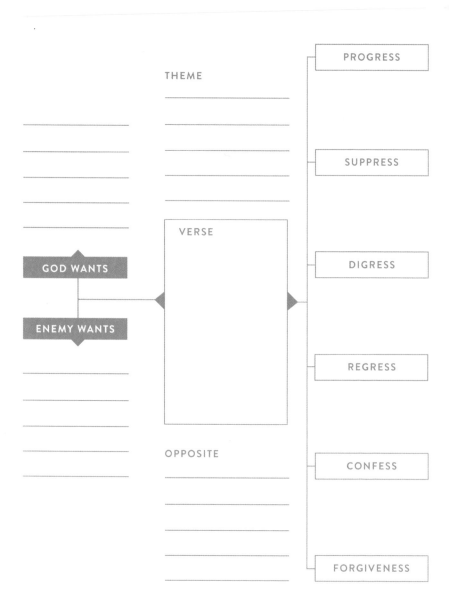

THEME

PROGRESS

SUPPRESS

VERSE

GOD WANTS

DIGRESS

ENEMY WANTS

REGRESS

CONFESS

OPPOSITE

FORGIVENESS

Find more printable worksheets of this Bible study exercise at proverbs31.org/forgiveness.

As we close out this journal, I just want to leave you with one last thought.

In honestly assessing the resistance that I can definitely have in this process of forgiveness, especially when I've been deeply hurt, I think so much of it boils down to this: If I believe that I am the saint and the other person is the sinner, I'll never truly be able to see my own need for forgiveness. Therefore, I'll be much more resistant to give forgiveness. But, in reality, I can't keep assigning titles like "saint" and "sinner" when God simply calls us all to be servants. And, in being God's servant, I recognize forgiveness is the greatest gift He has ever given me. Because I desperately need forgiveness. And when I recognize my own desperate need for forgiveness, I'm so much more able to give it away freely and abundantly. My daily process now is to pray as the Lord's Prayer teaches us to pray:

> *"Our Father in heaven,*
> *hallowed be your name,*
> *your kingdom come,*
> *your will be done,*
> *on earth as it is in heaven.*
> *Give us today our daily bread.*
> *And forgive us our debts,*
> *as we also have forgiven our debtors.*
> *And lead us not into temptation,*
> *but deliver us from the evil one."* (MATTHEW 6:9–13)

What a beautiful gift. Forgiveness is made possible not by my determination but only by my cooperation with what the Lord has already done.

As God's forgiveness daily flows to me, I must let it flow through me. Lord, let it be so.

Every man has his secret sorrows which the world knows not; and often times we call a man cold when he is only sad.

—HENRY WADSWORTH LONGFELLOW

PRAY

Father, I desire to be a mentally and spiritually mature person who easily forgives and filters my feelings through the truth of Your Word. In my humanity, I get this wrong so often. Help me make emulating Jesus a daily part of the natural rhythm of my life. I am forgiven. Therefore, I must forgive. God, help me live this. Thank You for the forgiveness You've graciously and mercifully extended to me through Jesus. Help me extend the same measure to the people I come in contact with throughout my life. In Jesus' name, amen.

CHAPTER 1: FORGIVENESS, THE DOUBLE-EDGED WORD

1. Charlotte van Oyen Witvliet, Thomas E. Ludwig, and Kelly L. Vander Laan, "Granting Forgiveness or Harboring Grudges: Implications for Emotion, Physiology, and Health," *Physiological Science* 12, no. 2 (2001): 117–23, https://journals.sagepub.com/doi/pdf/10.1111/1467–9280.00320.

CHAPTER 4: HOW IS FORGIVENESS EVEN POSSIBLE WHEN I FEEL LIKE THIS?

1. Xue Zheng, Ryan Fehr, Kenneth Tai, et al., "The Unburdening Effects of Forgiveness: Effects on Slant Perception and Jumping Height," *Social Psychological and Personality Science* 6, no. 4 (2015): 431–38, https://journals.sagepub.com/doi/abs/10.1177/1948550614564222.

CHAPTER 5: COLLECTING THE DOTS

1. "Better Way to Deal with Bad Memories Suggested," ScienceDaily, April 18, 2014, https://www.sciencedaily.com/releases/2014/04/140418141121.htm.

CHAPTER 7: CORRECTING THE DOTS

1. Henri Nouwen, *Bread for the Journey: A Daybook of Wisdom and Faith* (New York: HarperOne, 1997), 210. For further reading on Henry Nouwen's 5 Lies of Identity, see *Who Are We? Reclaiming Our Christian Identity*.

CHAPTER 8: UNCHANGEABLE FEELS UNFORGIVABLE

1. Emma Seppälä, "Forgiving Others Literally Lightens Your Step, and 6 Other Ways Science Shows It Helps," *Washington Post*, March 30, 2015, https://www.washingtonpost.com/news/inspired-life/wp/2015/03/30/feel-lighter-jump-higher-the-science-on-how-forgiving-others-can-help-you-too/.

ABOUT THE AUTHOR

LYSA TERKEURST is the president of Proverbs 31 Ministries and the #1 *New York Times* bestselling author of *It's Not Supposed to Be This Way, Uninvited, The Best Yes,* and twenty-one other books. But to those who know her best she's just a simple girl with a well-worn Bible who proclaims hope in the midst of good times and heartbreaking realities.

Photo by Kelsie Garham

    Lysa lives with her family in Charlotte, North Carolina. Connect with her on a daily basis, see pictures of her family, and follow her speaking schedule:

> Website: www.LysaTerKeurst.com
> (Click on "events" to inquire about having Lysa speak at your event.)

    Facebook: www.Facebook.com/OfficialLysa

    Instagram: @LysaTerKeurst

    Twitter: @LysaTerKeurst

    If you enjoyed *The Forgiveness Journal*, equip yourself with additional resources at www.ForgivingWhatYouCantForget.com, www.LysaTerKeurst.com, and www.Proverbs31.org.

Proverbs 31
MINISTRIES

ABOUT PROVERBS 31 MINISTRIES

Lysa TerKeurst is the president of Proverbs 31 Ministries, located in Charlotte, North Carolina.

If you were inspired by *The Forgiveness Journal* and desire to deepen your own personal relationship with Jesus Christ, we have just what you're looking for.

Proverbs 31 Ministries exists to be a trusted friend who will take you by the hand and walk by your side, leading you one step closer to the heart of God through:

> Free *First* 5 Bible study app
> Free online daily devotions
> Online Bible studies
> Podcasts (You might find Lysa's Therapy and Theology
>   series very helpful as you continue your pursuit of
>   staying spiritually and emotionally healthy.)
> COMPEL Writer Training
> She Speaks Conference
> Books and resources

Our desire is to help you to know the Truth and live the Truth. Because when you do, it changes everything.

For more information about Proverbs 31 Ministries, visit

www.Proverbs31.org.

AN INVITATION FROM LYSA

When my family and I were trying to heal from the darkest season of our lives, I kept praying that we'd one day be able to use our experiences to help others find healing. But I didn't just want to do this at conferences. I've dreamed of inviting friends like you over to my home to break bread and share our broken hearts, face to face, heart to heart. So, I'd love to invite you to Haven Place—a safe space for you to find the biblical and emotional healing you've been looking for.

If you'd like more information on the intimate gatherings, Bible studies, and retreats we'll be having here, such as:

- You, Me & We: Stop Dancing with Dysfunction in Your Relationships
- Forgiving What You Can't Forget
- Moving On When Your Marriage Doesn't
- Practical seminars and intensives for those wanting to teach Bible studies with depth and clarity

. . . please visit lysaterkeurst.com/invitation-from-lysa.

I truly believe healing, hope, and forgiveness will be the anthem songs, prayers, and shouts of victory that will rise from this Haven Place.

Have you ever had lingering questions about forgiveness and moving on in the midst of hurt, like:

> What if it's not possible to reconcile the relationship? Do I still need to forgive?

> What did Jesus actually mean when he said to forgive 70x7?

> What if the other person never says they're sorry?

> In situations of abuse, what do we do about forgiveness?

You might be surprised and comforted by what the Bible actually says about each of these! Lysa TerKeurst has done deep theological research on these questions and more in her new book *Forgiving What You Can't Forget*.